Yes!
We CAN Turn This Nation Around!

A Practical Guide for Christian Political Involvement

By

Russell S. Hepler, B.A., M.A.R.

This book is dedicated to the Honor and Glory of the Lord Jesus Christ, the Author of Truth.

This book is further dedicated to all of the millions of average American patriots in this land who wish to see truth, freedom, faith, life, opportunity, and dignity restored to this great nation "of the people by the people and for the people."

May God continue to "shed His grace on thee"!

Yes! We <u>Can</u> Turn This Nation Around!

Introduction:

Look around today! What do we see? We see anxiety, fear, confusion, and discouragement. We see radical changes in our society, government, economy, schools, churches, and families. Much of what was "normal" just a generation or two ago is now considered outdated, bigoted, or ignorant. It's no wonder the average person feels completely overwhelmed and powerless.

But, that's exactly how those who are attempting to run our society want us to feel. "Don't pay much attention to things," they say. "Let the experts make the decisions. It's far too complicated for the average person to understand." "Besides, you're just one person. How can you possibly change the course of things? How can you ever make a difference?" Their rhetoric is designed to paralyze the masses and leave the elite in power to control the future. It is nothing new. It has happened repeatedly throughout the course of human civilization. Either it is one despot, or a small elite oligarchy of rulers who have sought to control the lives of as many people as possible. We'll talk more about what is going on now in our country in a later chapter.

Sadly today, too many Christians have retreated in to one of two camps. One group is getting more and more obsessed with the Lord's return. "Why worry about all the bad things we see going on around us?" They say. "After all, these are just 'signs of the times.'" "Jesus is due back any minute. He'll straighten out the mess." This group has given up trying to change the society. They are going into survival mode to wait things out until the end comes. Why do you think the false predictions of people like Harold Camping get so much attention? Many people hoped he was right. Some still believe in his constantly amended "prophecies."

The second group, which includes an alarmingly growing number of evangelicals, has basically queried, "What's so bad about socialism?" "After all, didn't Jesus command us to share with the poor?" "Why should some people get to be rich? Isn't it moral for them to have to give of their abundance to the poor?" This group looks at the growing societal trends as ultimately good for us all. Won't equalizing income make for a better society? They have failed to understand the Bible and what it says about work, wealth, charity, and the difference between the roles of the Christian, the family, the Church, and the government.

Neither group has it right. To align with either group will lead to personal and national disaster! There are clear Biblical teachings on all of these areas. We will explore them briefly in a later chapter. But, suffice it to say that there is a strong Biblical message to every Christian today as to how to fix all of the major economic, social, and government problems we see today.

"Well, that's easy for you to say!" "I'm only one person with limited time and resources." "How can I possibly make a dent in any of these areas?" "Even if I thought I could help to change things, how would I know where to start?" I've heard those statements and questions many times. My response is what this book is all about. It is my firm belief that every individual person can make a huge difference in the future of our society. It only takes a bit of basic training and motivation to turn even the most uninformed, but concerned person, into a powerful "warrior" for change!

Yes, that's right! You are a potentially powerful warrior for change! The power each of us individuals still has in this society is far greater than anyone has led us to believe. Some of our leaders are content to keep us in ignorance – that makes us easier to control. Still others are ignorant themselves of our history, of the Constitution, and of what the Bible really teaches about being a good Christian citizen. But, ignorance is far from "bliss." It is destructive. It is debilitating. It is discouraging.

This book is a both a foundational rationale for our involvement as well as a practical guide as to how to be effective in our efforts to change things for the better. I certainly don't have all the answers. But, what I have learned personally, professionally, and through the advice and resources of others, I share with the reader. Please take and use this information and inspiration as best fits your circumstance. Please learn from my many mistakes as well as my successes. And, may the Lord bless you as you seek to serve Him in this time and in this place in history!

Chapter 1: We've Been Lied To!

"Christians should not be involved in politics." "We have a Separation of Church and State which keeps religion from influencing government." "America was founded by men who were largely Deists and Enlightenment Humanists." "The influence of Christianity on America has been minimal." "Radical fundamentalist Christian extremists want to turn America into a theocracy." "Christians are largely poor, uneducated, and easy to command." "Real Christians should not entangle themselves in political affairs, but concentrate on saving souls." "Fundamentalist Christians are racist, sexist, homophobic, bigots!" "America was founded by only rich, European, slave-owning men."

Okay, okay! I could go on and on with a long list of the lies I've heard about Christians and American government and history. Every statement I just listed is a lie being taught by large numbers of people today. Sadly, far too many people believe one or more of these lies.

There are many sources for these lies. We hear them in high school and college classrooms. We hear them in federal courtrooms. We hear them from pundits in the news media. Actors on TV and the movies spew them forth like gospel in "entertainment" that is far more indoctrination than anything else. Sadly, we also hear many of these lies from pulpits; from pastors who are either ignorant of history and Scripture, or who have sold their souls to left-wing liberation, pseudo-theology.

Far too many people sitting in the pews, the classrooms, or in front of computer screens, TV sets and movie screens, just accept these lies because they believe the messengers. They are either uninterested, uninformed, or even downright too lazy to examine the truth claims of these modern-day propagandists. It is easier to remain ignorant and just go with the flow. After all, aren't these lies what most people believe?

We Christians, though, have a very serious problem. **We are commanded to seek, teach, and live the truth in our lives. We cannot accept society's lies and live authentic lives for our Lord.** If we want to have any kind of spiritual health, we must constantly search out the truth. We must seek to teach the truth to others. And, we must model the truth to the world around us. There should be no room for falsehoods in any area of our lives.

We also have another, more difficult problem. We live in a post-modern era where consistency of thought and fact isn't necessary. Far too many people today say they believe one thing and then act quite the opposite. That's why slimy politicians can say that they are personally opposed to abortion while they vote to give millions and millions of tax dollars to abortion providers. That's why they can say there is a need to rein in government spending while at the same time slipping in "earmarks" for projects in their home districts.

It isn't just that people today are dishonest. They really have no moral compass. Whatever they want to believe, they believe no matter how inconsistent, silly, or stupid. These are the same kind of people that will donate thousands to "save the whales"; but will give next to nothing to stop famine in the third world. They believe those who kill baby seals and destroy eagles' eggs should go to jail, but those who kill babies in the womb are to be commended for their courage.

Yes, the world we live in today is filled with lies, liars, and advocates of the social benefit of lying. These are the people who said that Bill Clinton's perjury didn't count because he was just lying about adulterous sex with a "bevvy of bimbos!" They are the same people who equate slavery with the denial of homosexual marriage rights. They are the judges who have all but turned the Constitution on its ear to make it fit their social and political philosophies.

Amidst all of these lies, falsehoods, and propaganda we see a mass of humanity that no longer knows what to believe. Those of us who are committed to the truth really do have our work cut out for us. It falls to us to be so stubbornly committed to the truth that we will not be moved to compromise our faith and our lives. Yes, we need to teach the uninformed. Yes, we need to challenge the professional liars. Yes, we need to promote those who are based in truth, or at least who are seeking truth in what they do. And yes, we need to do battle with the "father of lies" for the souls of individuals and the culture at large.

But, our first step in doing any of these things is to be sure we know the truth before we begin. We must de-program ourselves from all of the lies we may have accepted over the years. We must examine afresh our faith, our history, and our understanding of a government "of the people, by the people, and for the people."

We cannot be successful if we attempt this without proper preparation. Those who will oppose our efforts will tear us to bits if we go off "half-cocked." **We must know what we believe. We must know why we believe it. We must know the most effective way to communicate our beliefs with others.** And, we must know how to defuse, refute, and turn back the arguments and the criticisms that will come our way from our opponents. They are well-entrenched. They have held their positions for decades. They have grown rich and powerful via their lies. They will not give up ground easily. They also will not play by any rules. They have no morality. Victory is all that matters for them.

For some of us, this discussion is a bit academic and philosophical; therefore, the amount of energy we may commit to it is limited by our spare time. For the left in this country, this is far more than philosophy. This is their livelihood. This is their ticket to power, fame, and wealth. And, since most of them are unencumbered by morals and ethics, achieving their goal is the only "good" they recognize. "Whatever it takes," is the motto they live by. If you doubt me on this, it will be to your peril and the peril of any effort you make.

Our struggle is literally life and death for millions. Here in America it is life or death for millions of unborn babies slaughtered in the womb. It is life or death for the thousands who die each year from suicide, drug addiction, STDs, and violent crime. In the rest of the world, it is life or death for millions who are deprived of basic food, medical care, stable government, and cheap energy.

You see, our faith isn't just a good idea. Christianity fleshed out into every area of a society results in the maximum prosperity for the maximum number of people in the world. We stand for the truth. The Scriptures reveal the truth. If its foundational base is allowed to support our societal efforts, the greatest good will come about. If society "exchanges the truth for a lie," then everyone suffers.

This is seen empirically in the results of removing Christian influences from our societal institutions. We have always had problems in our nation. That's to be expected in a fallen world, no matter how good our efforts. But, the problems we face today are so much greater than they were 50 years ago. What happened? The Church was undermined by heretical theology that denied the Bible as authoritative. The schools removed prayer and Bible-reading from the curriculum. Science claimed to be the "god" of the age. The government attempted to practice secular Christian charity to solve the problems of the poor and the family. Journalists became advocates for positions instead of objective news reporters. Hollywood threw off constrictions of content decency in movies and TV. And, the universities became the incubators of idealistic Darwinist Socialism.

Put all these things together and we have had a recipe for societal disaster that the world hasn't seen since the fall of the Roman Empire. Traditional churches have become radicalized and decline steeply as people flee their apostasy. Public education is a very expensive, inept, baby-sitting service that pushes young people through and out of their taxpayer-funded school doors regardless of ability or achievement. Real science has been replaced with hysterical "gloom-

and-doom" fanatics who scare people into poor economic choices and politicians into forking over billions in highly questionable grant money. The government has become more and more intrusive into every aspect of everyone's life; needing more and more control and money to justify its bloated, ever-expanding, existence. Real news doesn't exist anymore. The networks are filled with political hacks, celebrities, and celebrity wannabes. Hollywood keeps churning out mediocre garbage narcissistically labeled as "art." And, the modern American university system, once the envy of the world, is now little more than a caricature of political correctness ideology; conferring degrees on those who can't think for themselves, have very little ambition, but have huge senses of entitlement and even larger egos.

We have millions of able-bodied people receiving welfare. We have years and years of unemployment benefits with little or no requirements to even find work. We have politicians finding new rights in the Constitution to fit whatever they perceive will buy them votes in the next election. We have massive, unsustainable personal and governmental debt. We keep building more and more jails to house the growing criminal class. Those who simply want to work hard to provide for their families keep seeing their paychecks shrink and shrink.

Yes, when truth is abandoned, the lies mount and mount and form an ever-growing cesspool of quicksand that is trapping more and more people today than ever before in history. It is no wonder why people today give up hope and just go along with the system. They look around and see absolutely no real answers to their problems. Many people have just surrendered.

Okay, enough gloom! The purpose of this book is to discuss how to change things for the better. Following is material designed to encourage, instruct, and hopefully inspire you to learn, get involved, and make real changes in your corner of the world. **We don't have to be content with the status quo.** We don't have to feel overwhelmed with the lies we see and hear all around us. The real truth is that there are many more people out there who think and live like we do. We have been isolated and separated from each other for far too long. It is time we rise up together and work to transform our culture. This can't be done in one arena alone. It must be pervasive. The church must transform. The family must transform. Education must transform. And, of course government must transform. This book deals only with the government aspect of this transformation. Any lack of discussion of the other areas should not be taken to mean that they are unimportant. It just means they are beyond the scope of this book.

This process won't be quick or easily attained. It will require us to learn the basic Biblical facts concerning government and the basic historical facts of our nation. It will take soul-searching and much prayer as we seek to know where the Lord wants to place us in this battle. It will involve victories and defeats. We will feel times of great satisfaction and deep despair. We will make our share of mistakes along the way. But, persistence and faithfulness need to be our long-term goals. We will overcome in time if we don't give up.

That's the amazing thing about God's Truth. It will prevail eventually, no matter what. It is real. It describes things the way they can be. It will not fail. We must always be encouraged by these facts. And, **we must always remember – we don't fight this battle alone.** Heaven cheers when God's Truth is proclaimed. The Lord has promised to give us the gifts and abilities we need to do this. We will be amazed at the help that comes our way if we believe. So, onward! Let's prepare for victory!!

Chapter 2: What the Bible Really Says

We Christians use the Bible as our starting point in what we believe and how that dictates our actions. Therefore, it is only fitting that we begin our discussion of involvement with the Bible. What does the Bible say about government? Does it deal with this issue? Should Christians be involved in government? What is the Church's role in influencing government?

We'll look at these questions first here before moving on to further specifics. Space in this book will not permit an exhaustive study of all the Bible has to say about government and good citizenship. However, we will look at an overview of the Bible's teaching about the institution of government as well as some specific advice given about being good citizens. We will also discuss practical applications of these teachings for all Christians.

To begin our look, we'll start at the beginning – Genesis. Through the first eleven chapters of Genesis we see God create and guide the institutions of human society He established. In order from smallest to largest, they are: **Marriage** - Genesis 2:22-25; **Family** – Genesis 4:1-2, 25; **Community** – Genesis 9:1, 7; **Government** – Genesis 9:2-6; **Nations** – Genesis 11:7-9; and **Religion** – Genesis 8:20-21. None of these institutions is mutually exclusive. In fact, significant overlap is necessary and expected. But, each has their own distinct responsibilities and foci.

For our discussion in this book, we will focus primarily on two of them – government and religion (the Church). Today, our raging debate over "the separation of church and state" has been completely distorted from what God, and our Founding Fathers, originally intended. (We'll talk more about real American History in the next chapter.) Actually, the Bible does have much to say about the responsibilities of both church and government, their interaction, and areas they must not infringe upon each other.

The vast majority of human history has been dominated by one basic form of government – totalitarianism. Whether leaders were called kings, emperors, czars, general secretaries, or dictators-for-life, the structure was similar. Either one, or at most a tiny elite, controlled each society. Freedoms and rights were granted to the masses by those in charge and often at their whim. Power was held by force. Average citizens were little more than slaves to the leader or to the state.

When God set forth His covenant with the Children of Israel, he provided something far different. People often have two mistaken views of the form of government God set up for Israel. On the one hand, they describe early Israel as a theocracy. This is not true. A theocracy would have required an all-powerful priesthood that ruled the populace in the name of God. That was not the case. Yes, God did give His Law as a guide for civil, social, and religious life in Israel, but Israel also had civil authorities who were separate from the priesthood. (More on that in a moment.)

A second mistaken notion people have is that Israel was designed as a monarchy. After all, they say, just look at all the kings and queens they had: Saul, David, and Solomon, just to name three. But, God's plan for His people was to be a distinct nation from the rest of the nations of the world. When His people began to ask for a king, He tried to talk them out of it. He warned them that they would lose freedoms if they accepted a king's reign over them. Finally, when the people refused to listen to His prophet, Samuel, God commissioned Samuel to anoint Saul as the first king of Israel. Eventually, weak and bad kings led to Israel's division and destruction.

No, believe it or not, **God gave His people the right of self-rule**. Look at Exodus 18:21-23 and Deuteronomy 1:13-15. God tells Moses to select several levels of magistrates to manage disputes among the people. This was to provide for efficient civil government for the Tribe of Israel. In time, each tribal territory had its own leadership. When the leadership matched the character traits God told Moses to seek in each leader, the nation prospered. When people placed poor leaders over them, the nation suffered. Even after Israel had kings, each tribe still maintained some level of self-rule with a structure of elders and local leaders.

Another aspect of Israel's history that is often overlooked is **the concept of God-given rights that all people enjoyed**. Within the pages of the Pentateuch are described such rights as fair trials, private property, equal justice among most citizens, fair treatment of indentured servants and foreign nationals, punishments befitting crimes, personal responsibility for personal actions vs. family punishments, and a number of others. These were codified in the Sinai Covenant given from God. No beneficent ruler would have dreamed of stepping on them. God had guaranteed such rights to His people.

Now, that is not to say that Israel didn't have its share of malicious rulers who ignored and violated God's Law. But, usually these violations were in the context of a greater abandonment of God in general. When kings started worshiping the false gods of the region, then God's Laws were abandoned as well. When these things happened, God judged His people and brought calamity their way.

Both the Proverbs and the Prophets contain much advice for rulers and subjects. Bad rulers are criticized and condemned. Good rulers are encouraged and applauded. God was very interested in a just stable society for His people to live within. Some of this Biblical advice is repeated for the reader in the last chapter of this book.

One of the other things we learn by studying the Old Testament is the fact that religious and civil leadership were separate. Moses ran Israel's civil affairs. Aaron developed the religious priesthood. Both were important to the society. Both had their own responsibilities. Both supported each other's efforts. There was a form of "separation of church and state" then, but certainly not like the twisted interpretation coming out of our modern courts today.

In fact, **Israel's whole existence and success revolved around God**. Their goal was to honor Him with both their government and their religion. For them, there was no contradiction. There was no necessary restriction on religion's influence on the government. There also was no interference by government on religious practice. In fact, one glaring example of government seeking to usurp religion's responsibilities involved King Saul. In 1 Samuel 13 the account is told of Saul not wanting to wait for Samuel to come and offer a sacrifice to the Lord. Since Saul was impatient, he took it upon himself to act as a priest and offer the sacrifice, even though he was not a qualified priest. After the offering was concluded, Samuel arrived and condemned Saul for his sin. As a result, Saul would lose his throne and be replaced by David. God would not tolerate kings acting like they could disobey His Law whenever they felt circumstances warranted it. Saul's authority in Israel did not extend to the offices of the priests. When he crossed the bounds of government into religion, he violated God's established order. From that point on, his reign as king was doomed.

If we progress into the New Testament, we see a much different world established. By the time of Jesus, much of the known world was controlled by Rome. With Julius Caesar, Rome lost its semblance of a Republic. After him, Augustus ruled as a true emperor. During the years of the New Testament, Rome had absolute authority over all its territories, including the land of Palestine. Jesus ministered in this environment and carefully avoided seeming to take sides on either end of the political spectrum.

Jesus' primary purpose in coming to earth was to offer Himself on the cross as the sacrifice for the sins of all humanity. He led His followers to start the Christian Church. His goal was not political. If it had been, the movement would have been crushed under Rome's hobnail boots. Rome tolerated no dissent and allowed for no democracy. Jesus knew the world would only become transformed by a transformation of the human soul first. This was, and still is, the primary task of the Christian Church – to lead people to Jesus to set their souls free from sin and death.

Because of these facts, **Jesus made few overtly political statements**. In fact, His followers were made up of all sides of the political spectrum of the day. He successfully ministered to those who opposed Rome and to those who tolerated and compromised with her. One of Jesus' main political statements shows this as He avoided being "pinned on the horns of a dilemma" by his critics. In Matthew 22:15-22, Jesus has an encounter with the Pharisees. They were attempting to trap Him into committing to one or the other of the political extremes. The question arose about the poll-tax. Was it lawful to give it to Caesar or not? This was a Roman per capita tax assessed to every Jew. Here was the dilemma – if Jesus said no, He could be accused of sedition – inciting disobedience to Roman law. If He said yes, He could be accused of disloyalty to His own people. The Jews hated paying this tax to the Romans. This tactic used by the Pharisees – "pinning one on the horns of a dilemma" – was designed to make Jesus look bad no matter what He answered. It was one of those, "Have you stopped beating your wife yet?" questions.

Jesus' response showed both His unwillingness to be used as a pawn of the Pharisees and His agreement with God's order of both civil and religious institutions. He asked for one of the coins used to pay the tax. They brought Him the Caesar-inscribed Denarius. He forced them into a corner when He asked them whose likeness was on the coin. When they answered, "Caesar's", He had them defeated. Since Caesar's picture was on the coin, of course it was proper to give it back to him. But, Jesus also challenged their faith when He told them to give to God what is rightfully His as well.

Jesus was not an anarchist. God, in His Divine purpose, allowed Rome to become the dominant power in the world during Jesus' time. A multitude of reasons for that fact could be offered here, but space will not permit. Suffice it to say that Rome was used by God to grow the seeds of the Christian Church and the seeds of western civilization.

Jesus didn't seek to overthrow Rome. His plan was to transform it from the inside out. This is exactly what happened in the following centuries as Rome eventually became Christian. Even though the western half of the empire only lasted until the end of the fifth century, the eastern half of the Roman Empire blossomed into the Christian Byzantine Empire, which lasted for another thousand years.

Jesus completely agreed with the Old Testament idea that it is God who raises up and tears down kings and kingdoms. Look at His statement to Pilate in John 19:11. He made it clear to Pilate that his authority came not from Rome, but ultimately from God.

Perhaps the most detailed teaching in the New Testament about government is Romans 13:1-7. Here Paul gives an objective look at what God designed government to be and what each citizen's responsibility to government is. This is a general look at government, not a response to a particular situation. Because of that fact, we can be assured that what Paul is teaching here is a universal truth for Christians.

Please understand - Paul was not naïve. During his adult lifetime Rome had three of the worst Caesars in its history in succession. I'm speaking of Caligula, Claudius, and Nero. Caligula was insane, inept, and incredibly perverse. He eventually was assassinated by his own Praetorian Guard. Claudius was weak and ineffective. He was also anti-Semitic. Both the Bible and history record his expulsion of all Jews from the city of Rome. Nero was self-obsessed and insane. He instituted the first Roman persecution of the Christian Church. Both Peter and Paul were martyred during his reign.

So, when Paul talks here about what government is supposed to be, he understood fully what bad government looked like. Despite the fact that Rome had lousy emperors then, Paul still was not advocating anarchy or revolution. Now, it is very true that Paul lived under a vastly different political system than we do today. (We'll discuss those differences and how they apply today later.) But, first, let's take a bit of an in-depth look at what Romans 13 is teaching us.

Romans 13:1-7 – A Brief Bible Study

[1]Every person is to be in subjection to the governing authorities. For there is no authority except from God, and those which exist are established by God. [2] Therefore whoever resists authority has opposed the ordinance of God; and they who have opposed will receive condemnation upon themselves. [3] For rulers are not a cause of fear for good behavior, but for evil. Do you want to have no fear of authority? Do what is good and you will have praise from the same; [4] for it is a minister of God to you for good. But if you do what is evil, be afraid; for it does not bear the sword for nothing; for it is a minister of God, an avenger who brings wrath on the one who practices evil. [5] Therefore it is necessary to be in subjection, not only because of wrath, but also for conscience' sake. [6] For because of this you also pay taxes, for rulers are servants of God, devoting themselves to this very thing. [7] Render to all what is due them: tax to whom tax is due; custom to whom custom; fear to whom fear; honor to whom honor. (NASB)

[1]Every person is to be in subjection to the governing authorities. For there is no authority except from God, and those which exist are established by God.

Verse 1 begins with the civic responsibility of all people.

19

All are to be in submission to civil authorities. This is a universal statement by Paul. This means all people, not just Christians.

Paul gave this statement also to correct any bad thinking on the part of Christians that they only need to submit to Christ vs. human institutions.

The Greek word - "subjection" – used here is a broader term than to obey – it literally means "to stand under." Christians "stand under" government in the scheme that God has instituted for ruling the world.

The words - "governing authorities" – mean any person who represents the power of the state – from local on up.

But, subjection here does not imply inferiority. The believer is subject to the state, not because the state is better, but because the state has responsibilities the believer does not.

A second concept clearly enunciated here is that all civil authority comes from God. God delegates His authority to government.

Here Paul is stating the divine ideal, not human reality. But, the principle espoused here is valid even when malevolent rulers reigned. As stated previously, Jesus reiterates this truth to Pilate as He stood before him – John 19:11- authority comes from above.

God has ordained government as the institution to carry out His judgments in this world.

Paul also understood that it was also critical for Christians in Rome to be good citizens in light of the recent past problems with the Jews and Claudius.

² Therefore whoever resists authority has opposed the ordinance of God; and they who have opposed will receive condemnation upon themselves.

Verse 2 states that those who oppose civil authority are really opposing God.

The phrase - "He who resists" – literally means "sets himself in array against" – a military image of opposing armies standing ready to fight each other. If one refuses to obey the government, it is as if he is at war with God.

The word - "condemnation" – carries the idea of a judicial sentence. He is judged as guilty. Condemnation results from either personal or societal anarchy.

³ For rulers are not a cause of fear for good behavior, but for evil. Do you want to have no fear of authority? Do what is good and you will have praise from the same;

Verse 3 describes the civic responsibility of rulers.

Rulers exist to promote good behavior. Civil government is God's servant in rewarding good and punishing evil.

Paul is making an assumption of the moral "rightness" of government. The Greek word - "right" - means "good" – *agathon*. If we do "good", government will be on our side. We will have no reason to fear government if we do "good."

⁴for it is a minister of God to you for good. But if you do what is evil, be afraid; for it does not bear the sword for nothing; for it is a minister of God, an avenger who brings wrath on the one who practices evil.

Paul then goes on to describe that rulers are ministers of God in verse 4.

Two Greek terms are used in this passage for rulers being ministers of God:

> Verse 4 – *diakonos* – used two times – means servants – similar to ministers of the Gospel.
> Verse 6 – *leitourgoi* – means priest and public official.

These are used to imply the ministry nature of public service. Rulers are like ministers and priests, but in a different arena. They still exist to serve God. The ruler, like the priest, discharges a divinely ordained service.

Government is a way to serve God by encouraging righteousness and repressing crime.

(Elected officials need to see themselves in this way.)

Rulers exist to punish evil.

The Greek word - "Wrong" - means "evil" – *kakon*.

The verse goes on to describe government as bearing the sword. "Bear the sword" - means carry or wear the sword.

The sword was the symbol of the Roman magistrate's imperium. Magistrates either carried or had carried before them a sword to symbolize the power of life and death they held in their hands. It is clear that, at least in the Roman world, this meant execution for some crimes.

In this power to punish evil, the state is charged with a function which has been explicitly forbidden to the Christian and the Church.

Government is to avenge evil. Evildoers are right to fear government. They will receive wrath for their misdeeds.

5 Therefore it is necessary to be in subjection, not only because of wrath, but also for conscience' sake.

The Civic Responsibility of Christians is further described in verse 5.

Being in submission to rulers is part of our submission to God. We are in submission not only because of the fear of wrath if we disobey, but also for the sake of our consciences.

Because we understand that God has appointed rulers, we must submit to them. All Christians should be model citizens since we understand that government gets its authority from God.

6 For because of this you also pay taxes, for rulers are servants of God, devoting themselves to this very thing. 7 Render to all what is due them: tax to whom tax is due; custom to whom custom; fear to whom fear; honor to whom honor.

Verses 6-7 explain why rulers deserve our support financially.

Paul's focus on taxes is a focus on the need to pay government officials' salaries. They deserve to be supported because they devote their lives to service.

We are to give rulers all their due: taxes, customs duties, respect, and honor. Various types of Roman taxes are represented here.

Rulers also deserve the people's respect (fear). We are also to honor rulers for their office.

Paul mentions one additional responsibility of Christian citizens in 1 Tim. 2:1-2 – pray for those in authority.

In the course of this look at the Scriptures, a question comes flying at us at this point – **"Who Is Caesar?"** We know in Paul's world, power was clearly defined. It flowed from the top down. It was also not debatable or changeable for the average citizen. But, we live under a much different system. So, for us today in America - "Who Is Caesar?" In our system of government, we **are** Caesar; or more correctly, we **elect** Caesar. Yes, that's right! We have been given the right to determine our own civil destiny in this country. We get to choose who we want to set over us in authority.

If we don't take this blessing and responsibility seriously, then we are disobeying God and will have lousy government. If we believe Romans 13, then we must be active citizens of the Republic. This ability to elect leaders is truly a blessing God has given us. But, He has also given it to us as a responsibility in living out our Christian faith.

A second question comes flying at us now as well – **"What happens when the ruler goes against the Law of God and demands his**

subjects follow him in sin?" What do we do when those in government promote evil instead of good? Do we simply go along and participate in evil because rulers are set in place by God? How do we respond when there is a clear contradiction between the Law of God and the laws of the land?

We American Christians have two choices available to us in this case. **First, we have the power to change evil laws and evil rulers every time an election rolls around.** If we passively accept evil laws, we are the ones who will be judged for our inaction. Unless we can say we have done all in our power to change bad laws and bad politicians, we have no excuse for the societal problems that exist. We are not called to anarchy, so we don't have the option of just ignoring the law. But, few Christians have "done all they can" to change bad laws. The point of this whole book is to explain what must be done and how to do it if we're going to turn this nation around. Until every Christian is an engaged citizen of the Republic, we have no right to gripe or wring our hands at the evil we see proliferating in our society.

Our second option is a much more extreme one, yet one that has been necessary in the past. That is **civil disobedience**. This also is not anarchy. If our consciences, based on our understanding of the Scriptures, tell us that a law is unjust, we are justified in disobeying it. In fact, if civil law goes against God's higher law, we have a duty to disobey it. But, if we do disobey law, we must be willing to suffer the consequences for that disobedience. We may have to suffer persecution to raise awareness for our moral stand. Scripture is clear in its praise of those who "suffer for righteousness sake."

This tactic of civil disobedience was a necessary one used by southern black Christian clergy in the civil rights movement of the 1960s. Southern segregation laws, though legally enacted, were morally wrong. All people are equal in God's eyes. In order to draw attention to the repugnant nature of these laws, it took the courage of many a committed Christian to stand passively, but forcefully against tyranny. Many were jailed, or worse, but eventually the bigots and racists were forced to give up these evil laws.

Submission to the law only goes to the point where the state requires disobedience before God. Whenever laws are enacted which contradict God's Law, civil disobedience becomes a Christian duty. We see this clearly described in Acts 4:18-21 and Acts 5:27-29. Two incidents are described concerning the conflict the apostles had with the Jewish Sanhedrin. In both incidents the apostles were ordered to stop preaching the Gospel. Their response in both cases was to "obey God rather than men." They refused to obey laws and authorities that were out of phase with God. They were also willing to suffer any consequences and persecution for that decision.

Following are a few more examples of Biblical civil disobedience:

> Exodus 1:15-22 – the Hebrew midwives disobeyed Pharaoh in not killing all of the male Hebrews babies.
>
> Daniel 3 - Shadrach, Meshach, Abed-nego disobeyed King Nebuchadnezzar and were thrown into the furnace.
>
> Daniel 6 - Daniel refused King Darius and was thrown into the lion's den.

Civil disobedience has also been employed by Christians in the pro-life movement. That was the tactic of groups like Operation Rescue back in the 1980s and 90s. Thousands of Christians quietly protested outside of abortion clinics across the country. Many were arrested for blocking entrances. No one in the movement was violent. Often, they quietly knelt in prayer. Many were terribly persecuted for their faith. I can still remember the footage of a cop kicking a kneeling man in the head. The radical pro-aborts used their political connections to attempt to have groups like Operation Rescue prosecuted using federal RICO statutes. How absurd! The purpose of RICO was to make it easier to convict members of the mob – organized crime in this nation. It was designed to put these murderers and racketeers behind bars, not to be used on those who were only trying to save innocent human lives.

People may disagree with civil disobedience as a method for political change, but there is solid Biblical basis to employ it if it is the only option left. However, as I said previously, we in the Church have not done all we can via the ballot box first to stop evil and immoral laws. **Until we can say, "we have done all legally within our power as citizens," then we dare not simply disobey laws we don't like.**

So, let's summarize our Biblical basis for involvement:

1. General Truths

- Christians are not anarchists.
- God will hold us accountable if we are not involved.
- We do not live in a monarchy where all decisions are made for us. God has given the responsibility of government to us.
- We must do all in our part to promote good government and change bad government.
- Whenever a ruler or law forces us to choose between the government and God; we choose God.

2. The Christian Ruler

- Public Service is ministry.
- Those who serve must have this attitude.

- We also must look at their offices as such.
- The good must be promoted.
- We need leaders who submit themselves to God in order to dictate their views, their sense of morality, and their efforts to enhance society.
- When we get mixed moral messages from our leaders, the whole of society suffers.
- Good leaders are sure about what they believe and can communicate those beliefs to the people they serve clearly and forcefully.
- Evil must be punished.
- Rulers must take law enforcement and civil defense seriously.
- The world we live in today is a dangerous place. Many would do all they can to destroy our way of life and our nation.
- Rulers must not tolerate crime, violence, and abuse of our citizens.
- Rulers must protect the citizens from all enemies, foreign and domestic.

3. The Christian Citizen

- Support of rulers is part of our faith.
- God expects it of us.
- It is part of living the Christian life.
- Keeping rulers accountable is part of our faith.
- We choose who rules us.
- We will have good rulers only if we are involved.
- We have the right to remove bad rulers – by law.
- Participation, as led, is part of our faith.

Here's what the late John R. W. Stott had to say on the matter:

> " . . . Christians, who recognize that the state's authority and ministry come from God, will do more than tolerate it as if it were a necessary evil. Conscientious Christian citizens will submit to its authority, honour its representatives, pay its taxes, and pray for its welfare. They will also encourage the state to fulfill its God-appointed role and, in so far as they have opportunity, actively participate in its work."
> (Stott. 1994. pp. 346-347)

Quite a bit more could be said about the Bible's position on government and Christian participation in government. But, I think you get the general idea – **Christians need to be involved.** Sadly, these truths have been mostly lost in our churches. People have avoided talking about the social, cultural, and political issues of the day because they don't want to be labeled as promoting the same "social gospel" as the liberal church does. Or, they have been ignorant of both the Bible's teaching and the history of Christian involvement in government in general and American government in specific. (The next chapter will deal with those truths in more detail.)

God gave us His Holy Word to guide our lives in every area. We must learn and employ His guidance in the arena of politics and government just as much as we employ it in our homes, our families, our churches, and our own spiritual lives. God's Sovereignty doesn't stop at the end of the church parking lot. This is His world. We are His children. He has given us a blueprint for all areas of our lives. **If we learn it and follow it, there will be no end to the miracles and blessings we witness.**

Chapter 3: What the Constitution Really Says

One of the main battles being fought today is over the history of the United States. Historical revisionism has taken hold of the History business and much of America's real history has been changed, omitted, or misrepresented in order to "sanitize" our history from its religious component and emphasis. This is all part of the secular socialist mission to devalue and convolute this nation's moral underpinnings.

The truth is – what has happened here in the American Republic is the most amazing story in all of human civilization! What our Founding Fathers created here has been the most successful nation and system of government ever devised. This nation has experienced more freedom, more prosperity, more peace, and more opportunity for more people than anyone else on this planet has ever known.

This nation – a Constitutional Republic, not a democracy – is unique in its lists of "firsts" among the world's nations. We have the world's first still-standing written Constitution. We have the world's first Bill of Rights – guaranteeing rights and privileges of citizens which no ruler may infringe. We used to have the world's strongest economy and economic system. We still have the world's strongest military. We have the world's first still-standing electoral system which guarantees a peaceful transfer of power after every election.

This was given to us for one simple reason. Our Founding Fathers, by vast majority, held one world view – Biblical Christianity. No, I'm sorry. They were not mostly Enlightenment Humanists or Deists as we are commonly taught. Deism may have grown in favor in England by the early 1800s. Enlightenment Humanism may have held sway in the French Revolution of the late 1700s. But, the truth is that neither philosophy gained wide acceptance in the American culture during the time of the Revolutionary war.

The truth is that in the years prior to the American Revolution it was the Christian revival of the Great Awakening that held sway across the colonies. Names like Jonathan Edwards, George Whitefield, Samuel Davies, Gilbert Tennent, and others were the ones everyone was talking about. **The hearts and souls of the soon-to-be nation were stirred by the Bible,** not the European secular philosophers we have been taught to glorify today.

Yes, God did, in fact, prepare minds, hearts, and souls for the sacrifice, privation, endurance, and future blessings that would come as a result of a hard-fought war and victory over the greatest military power in the world at that time. **Without Christian underpinnings, there would have been no victory and no America today.**

Leading up to the Revolutionary War, American pulpits flamed with talk of liberty and freedom. This was especially true of New England. But, all of the colonies were touched by these Bible-based cries for freedom. A famous story, now largely forgotten, is of Virginia clergyman John Peter Muhlenburg preaching a fiery sermon on independence and then, to put his faith into action, removing his preaching robe to reveal his Colonial officer's uniform and leading several hundred men of his congregation and community into the war's fray. This is just one story from ample evidence of The Christian Church's role in Independence. His statue, depicting this act, is visible in the U.S. Capitol.

I could go on and on with examples of Christians being involved from the very beginnings of colonization through Independence. Many others have already compiled such work. David Barton and *Wallbuilders* is a great resource. (Despite the current controversy over Barton's book – *The Jefferson Lies* – by questionable critics, I have found his work to be thoroughly researched and documented.) *Forged in Faith* by Rod Gragg provides a great overview of the significance of the Christian faith to America's first two centuries. Writers like William Federer and Peter Marshall have also written volumes about the real American History.

Real, undiluted, uncompromised historical facts show clearly that this nation was founded by people seeking to honor God with what was created here. Their primary source of inspiration was the Bible. Even their main secondary and tertiary sources also quote or allude to many, many Biblical passages.

Today, both the secularists and the liberal church are seeking to disguise these facts from the masses. Their goal is to sever our generation from our history so that we will not stand on our foundation to restore this nation. If the past doesn't matter or didn't really exist the way it has, then their idea of "change" can come about with far more ease. Karl Marx said, "Take away the heritage of a people, and they are easily persuaded." **And make no mistake; the governing philosophy of those on the political left of this country is secular socialism.** That is true even if some of their own disciples and advocates don't fully recognize it for what it is. Any political system that seeks to give government supreme authority over the lives of people is completely antithetical to everything our Founding Fathers created and passed along to us. **The heart of the American system is self-rule, not rule by the elite oligarchy of "experts" or professional politicians and bureaucrats.**

Let's take a brief look at our founding documents and see if this isn't true. First of all, let me emphasize that **our founding documents were given for the people, not just the academic elite or the federal courts to read and interpret.** These are for all people to read, study, know and implement in our society. We cannot believe the lies being told today by the leftist elitists that we "common folk" are just too stupid to understand what they really mean. If people today don't know and understand our founding documents, it is because the government school system, fraught with socialist indoctrination, has failed miserably to teach the truth about them. We used to live in a time when every school child had memorized most of these documents as part of their education. Now, the average high school graduate can't even tell you much about Lincoln, let alone recite his Gettysburg Address!

"IN CONGRESS, July 4, 1776.

The unanimous Declaration of the thirteen united States of America,

*When in the Course of human events, it becomes necessary for one people to dissolve the political bands which have connected them with another, and to assume among the powers of the earth, the separate and equal station to which the **Laws of Nature and of Nature's God** entitle them, a decent respect to the opinions of mankind requires that they should declare the causes which impel them to the separation.*

 ***We hold these truths to be self-evident, that all men are created equal, that they are endowed by their Creator with certain unalienable Rights, that among these are Life, Liberty and the pursuit of Happiness.**--That to secure these rights, Governments are instituted among Men, deriving their just powers from the consent of the governed, --That whenever any Form of Government becomes destructive of these ends, it is the Right of the People to alter or to abolish it, and to institute new Government, laying its foundation on such principles and organizing its powers in such form, as to them shall seem most likely to effect their Safety and Happiness."*

(http://www.archives.gov/exhibits/charters/declaration_transcript.html) (Emphasis mine)

This excerpt from the Declaration of Independence shows quite clearly that our Founding Fathers understood that human rights come not from any king or state, but are a gift of God. It is obvious in reading the Declaration that our founding fathers understood that God was the author of all human rights.

> - These unalienable rights came from God, not bequeathed from any "state."

- They further asserted that to secure these rights, governments are instituted among men.

- This assertion agrees with Romans 13 – the state gets its authority from God.

- Further, they also assert that civil disobedience and revolution are legitimate responses if the state attempts to take away our God-given rights.

As the Declaration goes on, the document lists 27 reasons for separating from Great Britain. We usually only hear, "no taxation without representation" today as the reason for the Revolution, but they had far more grievances with King George III than that.

A simple, straightforward reading of the Declaration makes it clear that they believed they were in God's will in calling for Independence. They rejected England's abuses of their rights and declared that because of those abuses, the British government had forfeited its authority over their lives. These 56 men who signed this document knew the possible cost to them for committing an act of open treason against the British crown. It was not just poetic language they used to close the document when they stated, "And for the support of this Declaration, with a firm reliance on the protection of divine Providence, we mutually pledge to each other our Lives, our Fortunes and our sacred Honor." They all knew that if they failed, they would all lose all three – lives, fortunes, and sacred honor.

After a long war, America was born. But, exactly what was America? At first, it was a loose confederation of independent colonies without a strong central government. The Articles of Confederation were adopted to unite the colonies together. But, they were too weak to have any real meaning. So, a Constitutional Convention was called, again to Philadelphia, in 1787. By September of that year a new form of government was birthed – the United States of America – a Constitutional Republic. Notice how it begins:

"We the People of the United States, in Order to form a more perfect Union, establish   Justice, insure domestic Tranquility, provide for the common defence, promote the general Welfare, and secure the Blessings of Liberty to ourselves and our Posterity, do ordain and establish this Constitution for the United States of America." (http://www.archives.gov/exhibits/charters/constitution_transcript.htm l)

- The new nation of America created the world's first written Constitution which spells out the limitations and responsibilities of the government.

- It was, as indicated by the opening of "We the People", a document of the people of the United States spelling out what kind of government they would submit to obeying.

- They state that the purpose of the government of the US was six-fold:

> To form a more perfect union
>
> Establish justice
>
> Insure domestic tranquility
>
> Provide for the common defense
>
> Promote the general welfare
>
> And secure the blessings of liberty for posterity

- All of these ideas ring true to what Paul says in Romans 13.

Here is what Chief Justice John Marshall would later say about the Constitution:

"The people made the Constitution, and the people can unmake it. It is the creature of their will, and lives by their will." (Chief Justice John Marshall, 1821)

http://www.archives.gov/exhibits/charters/charters_of_freedo m_8.html

The Constitution created three branches of government – Legislative, Executive, and Judicial – in that order. It further created a two-chamber legislature, a secondary executive office – the Vice-President, and made provision for further levels of federal courts. It described a system of checks and balances to make sure no one branch of government could dominate the others. It also allowed for a federal system – making sure state and local governments had jurisdiction over the areas not enumerated for the national government.

As good as the Constitution was, there were some delegates who still feared the loss of individual rights of citizens from this new government. From that concern grew the Bill of Rights – the first ten amendments to the Constitution. It is clear to all that the first and foremost right people were concerned about was freedom of religion. It is the very first right enumerated in the very First Amendment to the Constitution:

"Amendment I

Congress shall make no law respecting an establishment of religion, or prohibiting the free exercise thereof; or abridging the freedom of speech, or of the press; or the right of the people peaceably to assemble, and to petition the Government for a redress of grievances."
(http://www.archives.gov/exhibits/charters/bill_of_rights_transcript.ht ml) (Emphasis mine)

A few things to note about the first Amendment:

- **It applies to Congress.** Congress shall be prohibited from the clauses that follow. That's because our Founding Fathers saw the responsibility for creating law to be in the hands of Congress. The Executive Branch and the Federal Courts had different roles in the application and interpretation of the laws Congress created, but it was Congress (the representatives of the people) who was to create law for this nation. Notice, there is nothing in here that talks about regulating agencies, arbitrary federal judges, and unelected "Czars" having authority to make law.

- The first two clauses of the First Amendment deal with religion. Respectively, they are known as the "Establishment Clause" and the "Free Exercise Clause."

- The phrase "respecting an establishment of religion" has been totally warped by our modern courts. Simply put, this clause means that Congress shall not recognize or endorse any one of the "established" religious denominations as the colonies had recognized them. An "established" religion was the official denomination of a colony. For example, in Massachusetts the "established" religion was Puritan Congregationalism. In Virginia, the "established" religion was Anglicanism. **Our Founding Fathers wanted no national church; no official American denomination.** In the colonies with "established" denominations, those other denominations that existed were known as "dissenters." Groups like the Baptists and the Methodists were among the dissenters in places like New England and Virginia. The spelling word we all learned in school – antidisestablishmentarianism – is related to this issue. Antidisestablishmentarianism was the political position to oppose the removal of established denominations in colonies. In other words, this was the position to keep established denominations in the colonies.

- The Free Exercise Clause clearly states that the Congress had no right to interfere with anyone's chosen religious practices. This component of the First Amendment has clearly been ignored or diminished by the Federal Courts over the years.

- **Please also note that the phrase "separation of church and state" does not exist in the First Amendment!** It does not exist anywhere else in the Declaration of Independence, the Constitution, the Bill of Rights, or any of the subsequent amendments to the Constitution.

- The phrase "separation of church and state" came from a private letter written by President Thomas Jefferson in 1802 to the Danbury, Connecticut Baptist Association. It was in response to their letter of concern sent to him. They were worried about their right to practice their religion being infringed by the government of Connecticut since it was dominated by Congregationalists. Jefferson gave his opinion that they needn't worry about government interference of their religious practices because the First Amendment had "erected a wall of separation between church and state." That wall would prohibit the government from telling people which church they needed to join or worship within. In other words, Jefferson's opinion, not an official Presidential proclamation, was that the government had no right to interfere with someone's religious practice.

- From the ratification of the Bill of Rights in 1791 until 1947, that was how the U.S. courts also interpreted the First Amendment. America truly had religious freedom in this period. But, since then several rulings and laws have eroded this freedom to almost nothingness.

Following is a time line and brief sketch of the events which have eroded our First Amendment rights in this nation:

1947 – Everson vs. Board of Education (Change Came)

- For the first time, the Supreme Court took "separation of Church and State" out of context in a ruling.

- In fact, the court, with no precedent, turned its meaning around 180 degrees.

- It found that religion had no place in government.

1954 – The Johnson Amendment

- Then Senator Lyndon B. Johnson from Texas attached an amendment to a bill which became law that prohibited any 501c3 charitable organization from making any political statements. Since most churches are incorporated under 501c3 rules, this effectively stifled all political speech in churches.

- Johnson pushed this amendment because he was tired of the criticism coming at him for his political corruption from the pulpits of Texas pastors.

- His amendment passed with support from other southern Democrat Senators who wanted to silence the southern black civil rights preachers. These racist southern Senators wanted to keep segregation the law of the land. If they could silence the preachers via this law, they thought, then the civil rights movement would fail.

1962 – Engel vs. Vitale (Supreme Court Decision)

- This ruling banned prayer in public schools.

- The court, for the first time, reinterpreted the First Amendment to interpret "Church" as religious activity rather than an organized denomination.

- In effect, it stated that the government was to be separate from religious activity as opposed to prior understandings that the government would have no national denomination.

1971 – The "Lemon Test" (Supreme Court Decision)

- So called because the case was Lemon vs. Kurtzman.

- It set up a 3 prong test to insure that any public religious activity had to have a "secular" purpose in order to be legal.

- Obviously, the test is heavily weighted in favor of secularists and discriminated against people of faith.

1985 – The "Endorsement Test" (Supreme Court Decision)

- This ruling basically stated that the government can't even appear to be "friendly" to religion or it has violated the First Amendment.

1992 – The "Outsider Test" (Supreme Court Decision)

- This ruling gave religious minorities the right to halt the public religious activity of others they disagree with.

- Essentially, an "atheist" can stop public prayer because he is "offended" by it no matter how many people want it.

This timeline shows clearly that the First Amendment has been totally butchered by the courts over the past 70 years. Its original intent was to protect everyone's right to freedom of religion without any interference from the government. **Simply put, the First Amendment was intended to guarantee two things. There would be no state church in America. There would be no control of the churches by the government.** Our Founding Fathers had seen the abuses of both extremes in Europe. In Great Britain, the church was subordinate to the state; the king/queen being the head of the church. In the Holy Roman Empire, the state was under the authority of the church. Papal authority superseded temporal authority.

Instead, our Founding Fathers used a Biblical model for the relationship of church and state. Both were ordained of God. Both were necessary for the success of society. Both were to support and aid each other's efforts. And, both had their distinct roles and functions. **What our Founding Fathers gave us in the First Amendment was in complete agreement with Romans 13.**

There was no restriction placed on religion by the government. In fact, the early American Government was indeed very friendly to the Christian religion. The Congress approved and paid for the creation of an American printing of the Bible. They also authorized moneys for Christian missionary efforts to Native American tribes. Jefferson and others write about attending Sunday Christian worship services in both the newly built U.S. Capitol and U.S. Treasury buildings. President

41

George Washington's first Thanksgiving Day Proclamation in 1798 was very Christian in its tone and content. It most definitely does not use the language a Deist would use! Unlike Jefferson's private letter to the Danbury Baptists, Washington's Thanksgiving Day Proclamation was an official document of his office. It was also approved by Congress.

Another example of our Founding Fathers approval of the Christian faith is the fact that John Jay – the first Chief Justice of the Supreme Court – also became one of the first presidents of the American Bible Society. He had none of animosity to Christianity we see today on the Supreme Court.

My points through this chapter are very plain. **Our heritage in this nation is firmly entwined with Christianity.** To deny this reality is to either be uninformed or have a secularist agenda to destroy our heritage and history. It is only over the past 70 years or so that this has been changed by a small number of elitists who have taken power away from the people and attempted to impose their world view of a secular socialist utopia on this nation. This effort has done nothing good for this nation. The problems we face today are ever-growing exactly because we have secularized this society.

If we want to turn this nation around, we must rediscover our roots and our heritage. We must teach the truth about our history to everyone who will listen. We must learn it ourselves first. We have a great, solid foundation of faith upon which this nation rests. **All who call themselves Americans must know this truth if we are to remain a free people.**

Chapter 4: What If I Don't Have Much Time and Money?

The world today is a hectic place. Our lives are filled with so much necessity that we seldom get a chance to catch our breath. For me to ask you to take on something extra could be considered downright rude! After all, how can we possibly fit any more things into an already overburdened schedule?

But, yes, I am asking you to consider involvement in politics and government. It does need to become somewhat of a priority in each of our lives if we want there to be any kind of future for our children and grandchildren. **We are on the edge of a precipice today.** It won't take much more for our nation to plunge off into the chasm of chaos and crash onto the rocks strewn with the remnants of other failed societies of the past. Yes, we must get involved if we want to avert disaster. Yes, we must start looking to what it is we can do to change the course of our nation. The promised socialist utopia is rapidly becoming an eerily similar totalitarian nightmare that other nations have experienced.

My purpose here is not to make anyone feel guilty. I'm certainly the last person to ignore the present realities of hectic modern family life. My goal here is to provide information and encouragement to everyone to get involved at whatever levels your time, pocketbook, and interest allow. Not everyone has to quit their job and run for office in order to change things. **There is something for everyone to do.** Together, we'll explore the options and give you choices that fit your family's schedule and budget.

Let's talk first about time management. **Do you think you could find one hour a week to give to this effort?** It need not be all at once. You could break up the time as the schedule allows. Now, I know what you're saying, "How can I possibly make a real difference if I only give an hour a week to the effort? Don't I have to commit much more time than that to make it work?" The answer is – "No." If every Christian in this nation got involved one hour per week in participating in our government, we would have a radically different nation.

Let me illustrate. In one hour, you could make dozens of phone calls urging people to vote. You could send a couple dozen brief emails to elected representatives, urging them to vote a certain way on pending legislation. In one hour, you could create a list of preferred candidates, make copies, and give them to friends and family as you see them. In one hour, you could take a drive through your community, putting up signs for your favorite candidate. In one hour you could take a brief shift outside a polling place handing out literature for your candidate. In one hour you could check the latest info from activist websites of your choice and forward them on to those on your contact list. In one hour your prayer group could pray for all of those in government that you can think of. In one hour you could teach a Sunday school class about basic civics from a Biblical perspective.

I could go on and on with examples, but I think I've made my point. **It doesn't require much time to make a huge impact**; especially if you compound that time commitment with all of the others in your church. Imagine a church of 100 giving 100 man-hours per week to changing this nation! At the end of the year, your church alone would be responsible for 5,200 hours of activism!! Now, multiply that by all of the Bible-believing churches in your area and multiply that number by all the Bible-believing churches in your state and - WOW!! - You have a full-fledged revolution on your hands the likes of which this nation has never seen. I guarantee you if we could approach those numbers, this nation would be totally transformed. I also guarantee the vast majority of those serving in government would be very, very responsive to what *We The People* want!

Our problem today is the fact that a tiny minority of people are calling the shots in our nation. Because of our inaction, they can get away with it. That's why those in office get swelled heads and fat bank accounts. No one is really paying attention to what they are doing.

When the light of truth is shone on them and their actions, most cannot stand long in the spotlight. Our involvement is the only accountability they are likely to ever have.

So, let me rephrase the question – Do you have an hour a week to change the world? I think if you look hard at your priorities and current time usage; the answer will be a resounding, "YES!!"

Now, let's move on to another topic. It has been said that "money is the 'mother's milk' of politics." That is all too true. Rich people, who want to influence elections and legislation, put out large sums of money to see things happen their way. We may not be able to compete with them one on one, but we can make a serious contribution to the process if we do our part. Even if we can only give a few dollars a week, we can be part of a vast army that is able to fund every effort we set our minds to growing. Many good ministries and organizations already exist to fight the battles we can't fight alone. Their effectiveness in bringing about change is definitely related to how well funded they are. That's where we come in.

Once again, let's look at the numbers. If you are able to give $20 a month to various organizations, that comes out to $240 a year. If everyone in your church of 100 members does likewise, that's an impressive $24,000! Imagine if 100 churches of your size commit to doing the same thing. **The total is an amazing $2,400,000 a year!** How much change do you think could happen if worthy organizations had that kind of funding? Remember, this is possible for a commitment of less than $5 a week. Can you spare a five dollar bill each week to help save this nation? Let's face it; most of us probably go through that much change each week that we never miss.

Yes, we can make a big difference even if we aren't rich. We just need to commit together to work for a common goal. No one needs to bear a large portion of the load. Everyone can be a part of what's happening without radically changing our present lives. **There is nothing the people of God can't do if they come together.**

If time and resources are tight, there are ways to maximize efforts using minimal resources and time. For one thing, you can plan your activist activities to coincide with family projects. What a great civics lesson for our kids. Every once in a while family day could be handing out literature for candidates. On the way to visit the local ice cream shop, take a few candidate signs along to put out. Make it a school project (especially if you home school) to do research about elections and activist groups you might consider supporting and drawing information from. Take the family to a rally. Make your own signs to display. All of these examples are easy and doable for the average family. They also make a big difference without much effort.

If you have older children, or an older parent living with you, make your activism a family project with divided responsibilities. Get the "computer geniuses" in your family to do the research - finding things like voting records, activist groups, and monitoring credible news outlets for information. Have someone else compose letters or emails to be sent out when needed. Someone who has more free time can be the phone call person for the family. They can make contact with others before elections. They can call the local offices of elected officials to express opinions. **If everyone does a share of the tasks, then no one need feel overwhelmed.**

This practice can be expanded to include your church group of activists. By dividing the tasks, you have much more impact as a group than if you work as individuals. Besides, when you work as a group, you bring together diverse gifts and abilities. You are much more complete as a whole than as individuals. This church-related group also brings in the corporate prayer component to your efforts. Besides, the fellowship in such projects is usually very enjoyable, so this helps each of us spiritually as well.

A later chapter in this book will describe opportunities for involvement in greater detail. But, I felt it necessary to discuss time commitments first so that no one would feel overwhelmed at the scope of things that can be done. Remember, it doesn't take a full-time army to make this happen. **Everyone can make a huge dent with just one hour per week average.**

Keep in mind that you don't have to "reinvent the wheel" in your activism. Literally, there are hundreds of good groups out here working for change already. By tapping into their resources and getting involved with them at some level, you can multiply your efforts many times over. Decide which groups you want to support and aid with your time; then go to work changing your part of the world.

Please also understand that I am aware of how bad the economy is right now. My previous discussion about giving to groups was meant as an example of what is possible. If you just can't afford to contribute right now, don't worry. That may change some day. Also, if you are looking for practical advice about getting into a better financial position in general, I recommend the ministry of Dave Ramsey. He has books, seminars, a radio show, and a website all designed to help people improve their financial lot in life dramatically. By following his plan, you might be amazed at how much money you really do have!

Finally, **your mindset about this activism and support needs to be long term.** We could straighten out the current mess, get the nation back onto firm footing again, and feel like the crisis is truly over. But, if we quit after we feel we have won, twenty years from now we will be back in the same mess. This needs to be a permanent lifestyle change for us and our families. If we want to keep having a free America, future generations must stay involved as well. Remember, power abhors a vacuum. If we are not involved, someone else will come along to fill the void. This nation will either be run by decent, competent, moral people or it will be run by arrogant tyrants who will steal freedom at every turn.

Chapter 5: Where Do I Start?

This is a very common question for those who are new to political involvement. Truly, it can be daunting for the average person who is contemplating focusing their time and energy to help change our country. When we look around and see all that is happening in our country, most of it bad, it is easy to become quickly overwhelmed. But, don't despair! **There is a place for everyone to get involved, regardless of experience.**

The first place to start is with prayer. Ask the Lord what His will is for your involvement. Ask Him to lead you to discover your niche. Ask Him to guide you to information and people who will be able to assist you. Since I firmly believe God is raising His people up today to confront the wrong that is happening in our country, I believe He will guide you as to how you can join the massive force he is raising today.

The next step is one of education. I've touched on the Biblical foundations of good government. I've also briefly touched on the history of this nation and what our founding documents really say. Space in this book does not permit a more thorough understanding of each. However, many others have produced extensive information on these topics. Learning more about what our government was designed to look like and what God says about human government may well be a good starting point for involvement. This is just one type of education to which you may want to avail yourself.

Researching issues and issues' organizations is also helpful in finding your place in the movement. Learn more about the issues most important to you. Seek out organizations which are dealing with these issues. They should be able to give you both more background as well as practical steps you can take to become an active advocate for the issues.

One the political front, a good starting point is to **research who all of your elected representatives are**. From local to federal, it is important to know who it is that has been placed over you in authority. After you have created a list, then, as time permits, start researching who these people are. Find out what their voting records are. Find out which groups support them in office. Getting this "lay of the land" is an important early step to knowing what it is you want to do to help change the nation.

Don't allow yourself to be pressured to jump into activities before you feel ready. Politics is about always running from crisis to crisis. That's one of the reasons our nation is in the mess that it is in. Far too many people in government spend their time putting out societal "brush fires" without any long term planning or vision. We want lasting permanent change to happen, not just winning the next election. Take your time getting familiar with your issues and candidates and the system itself.

After you have achieved a comfort level of understanding, take the next step and inquire about involvement from issues groups, local political parties, or other groups out there working for change. A later chapter in this book describes a variety of options for you to explore. Wade in and get your feet wet with one or more of them. See which ones you like or prefer. And then, build your involvement accordingly.

Remember, you are a volunteer. **You can commit whatever time and effort you desire in this opportunity.** It may well be that you get involved with more than one group. It may well be that you may decide that the first groups you've joined aren't for you. We don't always know what God is doing. He may have us get involved with a group for just a season and then move us on to other things. Our purpose for working with a group may have only been to teach us the process. Or, perhaps He may move us on from a group that is going astray in its mission or is becoming ineffective.

My point is — there is plenty for everyone to do. Don't get discouraged if your first efforts end up being not what you wanted or expected. Move on and try something else. At one point in the late 80s and early 90s, I was heavily involved with our local pro-life group. But, over time I felt I wanted to be part of something that was broader. I respected the pro-life organization greatly, but I also sensed the need to advocate for school choice, fiscal responsibility in government, the preservation of the family, and other social issues. That desire led me to get involved with the Christian Coalition. They were absolutely pro-life, but they also advocated for a variety of conservative pro-family issues. For me, it was a necessary move to make. It wasn't that my passion to protect the unborn had waned; it was that my passion for other issues grew. I was growing in my development of involvement. I was glad I made the move, but I still greatly respect and admire those who exclusively fight for the unborn.

Another way to know where to begin is to ask friends and family who are actively involved what they did to begin. They may have good suggestions for you. By tapping into their experience, you can avoid wasting time with groups and politicians that may not be worth your time. They can also connect you with people who are active, or perhaps working full-time for change. **Networking is one of our strengths.** Word-of-mouth endorsements are usually reliable and helpful for our involvement.

It is also important to be practical in our initial involvement with any group or campaign. We will have to start at the bottom and do some "grunt work" at first. But, this can be a great benefit because it provides an opportunity to learn about the mission without feeling any of the pressures the leadership experiences. Even doing little things can be very helpful to those more actively engaged. Bringing coffee or snacks to office staff, stuffing envelopes, cleaning up after events, and other seemingly menial tasks can mean a great deal to the group or organization or campaign. Your efforts may not seem significant at the time, but you are part of the team working for change.

Individual work can also seem of little value, but that is far from the truth. Who knows how many "individuals" may have contacted a legislator about a certain bill. That quick email or two minute phone call may make a world of difference when put together with several thousand other ones. We may never know how much even small efforts may affect the whole. But, **we should never think that small efforts aren't worth doing.** Remember, it takes billions of grains of sand to make a beach!

My point in all of this is that there is no one right answer as to where to start. Do what seems practical and possible for you. You probably won't know your place in all of this activism until you have tried a variety of situations. When it feels right to you, it most likely is. When you begin to feel satisfaction in what you are doing, it's a good indicator that you have matched up your gifts with the mission needs. **Remember, the Lord is orchestrating all of this.** If you keep seeking His will, He will guide you to where He wants you and you best fit in.

So, get started, get involved, and explore your opportunities. You will be making a difference of some kind right from the beginning. Remember, before you got involved, there was one less person doing something to save this country. Now that you are involved, the army has grown by one more.   As God calls more and more people to action, those who are fighting for what we believe will be more and more successful. Each of us is part of that success. Each of us is part of the change that will happen. **If we don't quit or become discouraged, we will be victorious. God's Truth will ultimately be victorious!**

Chapter 6: Levels of Involvement – Something for Everyone!

Everyone is capable of making a real difference in some way. The following chapter is designed to help us explore where we fit in with our interest and our time and energy constraints. Let's break things down by categories. That may help us clarify what we want to accomplish in helping to save our nation and culture. For the sake of simplicity, we'll divide our involvement opportunities into three categories: **voting, issues,** and **politics**.

Voting:

Let's start first with voting. We may think that our one vote doesn't mean much, but **the right to vote is the backbone of our free society**. We citizens of America have a voice in all who are directly over us in authority. This right must never be minimized or taken for granted. Literally billions of people in history and in our current world have never known this kind of freedom and self-determination. It is a blessing from God that we have inherited by those who pledged "their lives, their fortunes, and their sacred honors" for us.

Registration:

Having said this, we must start first with the great tragedy of our time. Only about 50% of those eligible to vote in this country are even registered to vote! And, in a typical election, only about 50% of those registered actually vote. That's right! About 25% of adults are determining the fate of our nation each election. Those numbers do go up during Presidential elections. But, they also go down during local and state election cycles. In Primary elections, (if your state has them), the numbers are even lower. These numbers are pretty much the same for those self-identified as Christians. **Yes, even in our churches only about half of the people are even registered to vote!**

This, then, is the first and smallest level of involvement. Each of us must be registered to vote. It is simple, painless, and takes very little time to do. You just have to furnish basic information on a simple form, send it in to the relevant municipal or state agency, and you will receive a registration card or other form of voter ID. It may be necessary to research the specific voter registration regulations of your particular state so that you are clear how it works. But, the information is readily available. Often Post Offices and other government offices will have voter registration forms available. Some states even have automatic voter registration every time we renew our driver's licenses. It is possible to register online in many states as well. Check out voting regulations on your state's government website.

Given the levels of voter fraud over the past few elections, many states are tightening voting requirements to put an end to fraudulent and illegal voting. This is long overdue and absolutely necessary to preserve this precious right we American citizens have been given. Groups like ACORN are probably just the tip of the iceberg when it comes to voter fraud. We must support and applaud efforts by those in government to insure that, **in every election, the rule of "one citizen, one vote" is followed strictly**.

One of the choices that one must make when registering to vote is which political party to affiliate, or not affiliate with. Registering with a political party has certain advantages in many states. The main advantage is the ability to vote in Primary elections. Voters who are registered as "independent" will not be able to vote for candidates in Primary elections in states with "closed" primaries. The rule of thumb in Primary elections is that you only choose from among candidates of your own party. It's not until the general election that one may vote for any candidates running for a political office. That isn't true in all states and some states are currently changing the way they do Primary elections.

All too often the best candidates don't survive Primary elections because not enough of the people who agreed with their positions turned out to vote for them. This is one real way to have a huge influence over the direction of our country. We need to get good candidates through the Primary process so they will be able to run in the General Election. Since the turnout numbers are smaller, each vote has greater impact on the outcome. In other words, every registered voter who shows up makes a huge difference! This is all the more true with local elections. Very often a winner of a local Primary Election has defeated their opponents by only a couple dozen votes. So, being registered in the party of your candidate is absolutely essential to help them win a Primary election. The exception to this rule is what is known as an "open" Primary. States that have this allow people to select the party's ballot for which they wish to cast their vote. But, this makes being registered all the more important. If someone from another political party casts a vote for your candidate's opponent to help defeat your candidate, it makes the necessity of your voting for your candidate all the more important. It really isn't fair that people from opposite political parties should have any say about who their own candidate will face in the General Election. **Our involvement will keep the process more fair and honest.**

This is one of the tactics the Ron Paul campaign has used. Analysis of open Primaries shows that the majority of his votes don't even come from Republicans. He has chosen to run as a Republican, but doesn't have much Republican support. So, his campaign people are using loose voter registration rules to make it appear that he has far more support than he really does. Independents and even Democrats seeking to skew the Primary results have been his best supporters.

Voting:

After being registered to vote, the next step is to actually vote in every election. Remember, **there are no unimportant elections**. Everyone who has a political career, good or bad, started somewhere.

Most people don't run for President as the first political office they attempt. There are countless stories of people who came from humble beginnings who have worked their way up through the political system to gain national prominence. For some, it may have been that they started with being elected to a local school board or town council. It was in these small local elections that they learned how the political and campaign processes work. The got to know people and, more importantly, got known by their friends and neighbors. When they were ready to run for a higher office, they were experienced and had developed a base of support upon which to build.

For us, that means we need to be involved with every election. We may be starting someone's important future political career. We also may be instrumental in stopping someone who would be a lousy politician from beginning to cause us future problems. In my county, our current U. S. Representative used to be the County Sheriff. His father, who was County Commissioner at the time, helped to get him elected to this seemingly unimportant county-level job. But, several years later, when our U.S. House Rep retired, he was poised to run for that office. We joked about "Barney Fife goes to Washington", but he did win the election and has been in office for almost two decades now. He never does anything important. He stays in office by being fairly conservative on social issues and fairly liberal on economic issues. He never met a tax increase he doesn't like! He's entrenched with union support and probably won't be easily defeated by anyone. The citizens of our county have had to suffer with his third-rate leadership and lack of accomplishment for far too long. If he had been stopped when he first ran for sheriff, he would never have been heard of by anyone. He had no law enforcement experience then; just a father and grandfather who were well-connected politically. His family may have had future plans for him, but no one else saw what was happening in incubating his political career.

When we vote, we are doing our basic civic duty. We are fulfilling the basic requirement to maintain this incredible blessing God has given to our nation. We must always take it seriously. If our nation loses the basic freedoms those who came before us sacrificed, many with their lives, for us to have, it won't be because of some foreign invasion and overthrow of our government. It will be because we have given away our birthright due to our laziness and lack of commitment to generations yet unborn. All Christians must be taught this. All Christians must be urged to participate in the Republic at least at this level. **Ignorance and apathy are the real enemies of American freedom.**

This is all the more true when one considers just how much we could change the nation with this minimal effort by more of our people. Most elections are won or lost by a few percentage points; especially those that are hotly contested. The balance can be tipped by just a few percentage point swing in the votes or by just increasing the voter turnout by a small percentage. Yes, I guarantee you a much saner, freer America if even as many as 75% of Christians voted regularly. It won't take much effort. It doesn't require bundles of money. It doesn't involve vast amounts of time. It just takes the commitment of the Church to be the salt and light we are called to be in society in this arena.

Informed Voting:

"But, I don't know who to vote for." "I don't know which candidates to believe." These are common objections I've heard over the years. These go right along with the statement, "It doesn't matter; they're all crooks." None of these objections are legitimate, however. This is especially true today given mass media and the internet. It is relatively simple to become an informed voter. None of us wants to waste a vote on a candidate that either we know nothing about or a candidate that turns out to be the opposite from what they claim to be. We don't need to worry much about that anymore.

Today we have countless good issue-advocacy and candidate evaluation groups. It is simple to find out where candidates stand on issues; where they have been on issues they may have voted on in the past; and which ones are honest about their record and positions. We will talk more about these groups later on in this chapter. For now, suffice it to say that it is a simple matter to go into the voting booth with a firm grip on which the right and wrong candidates are. We can have confidence that our votes are meaningful with just a little work on our part. It need not be confusing, especially after our senses have been bombarded by a countless barrage of political advertising coming at us from all sides' right before an election. We can cut through the hype, rhetoric, and deception to see the truth of who the best people are to place over us in leadership. Yes, not only can we be regular voters, we can be confident voters!

Influential Voting:

One of the other questions I'm asked by people is how do we multiply our votes if we have severe limits on our time? Well, aside from places like Philadelphia and Chicago where one vote often suddenly becomes dozens, the rest of us can legally multiply our votes with just a minor effort. I like to call it influential voting. Once your family and friends know that you are someone who keeps up on politics, they will look to you for guidance. On the eve of an election, make a few phone calls and tell people who you're supporting and why. Most of them will thank you for making the choice easier for them. It may also serve as a reminder to them to vote the next day. If you reach a dozen people this way, you will have multiplied your vote by a factor greater than ten. Trust me; this is a good way to influence elections with little effort. In fact, **after a while, people will start calling you to ask who to vote for in an election**. Imagine if every church had about ten of these walking resources! Our influence would be huge in every community.

Make it your ambition to be the informed voting resource for your family, friends, and church. They will trust you and your opinions. As long as you give them good advice, they will continue to seek out your wisdom before each election. Since you will have become informed about the candidates for your own peace of mind, passing on what you have learned to others is a simple matter. If time permits, make a few extra calls and your influence will grow even larger. If you have a bit more time, make a list of good candidates and make copies to hand out to people you know. That way, they won't have to even try to remember all the names of the people when they are casting their votes. In some places, you can get facsimile sample ballots in advance of the election. If you can get some of these, you can mark them, make copies, and give them to people. They can then use them as a guide when they vote. Many of your family and friends will thank you for helping them participate in this way.

Issues Advocacy:

The next level of involvement focuses on issue advocacy. Every election is about important issues. Everything from life to gun rights to lower taxes plays in to whom we elect. It is, therefore, vitally important that we know where candidates stand on issues important to us. Will "Jim Smith" expand or restrict religious freedom if he gets elected? Will "John Doe" vote to only confirm judges who will adhere to the Constitution? Will "Mary Jones" vote for school choice? Does "Sally Brown" believe that life begins at conception? And, which groups are giving big money to "Bill Adams"' candidacy? All of these are important questions to ask and know the answers to before we vote in an election. The answers to all of these and many more questions are easy to find out. Advocacy groups for almost every issue are out there. Many provide voter guides and candidate evaluations. By receiving their information, it is easy to build a picture as to who the good and bad candidates are. A categorized listing of many of these groups is found in the back of this book.

Most of these groups are now high tech. It is a simple matter to click onto their websites and get the info we need. Some groups are multi-issue groups, so they will evaluate candidates on a number of issues. Others are passionate about their one issue. In either case, if they are doing their homework, they will be able to provide documentation as to why we should support or not support a particular candidate. Very often candidates who are on the wrong side of issues will refuse to answer candidate questionnaires from groups with which they disagree. This is especially true of liberal candidates when it comes to abortion, gay marriage, and gun rights. Some groups will just report this as "did not respond." But, a more thorough group will go the second mile at this point and evaluate a candidate on past public statements, or past voting records if they are currently in office. This is the kind of info we need since sadly, politics has its share of the dishonest.

Church Issues Advocacy:

If you are passionate about a particular issue, or issues, you could become a contact person for one or more groups. By getting involved with them, they will rely on you to get their information out to those around you. This is vital, especially in churches. **Every church should distribute non-partisan voter guides before every election.** It is perfectly legal. In fact, I would argue, that it is the moral thing to do. Every voting Christian should be assured that their vote will be cast for people who agree with our faith and its moral teachings. For example, no one wants to unwittingly vote for a stealth pro abortion candidate. That makes us somewhat of an accomplice to abortion if we help to elect such a "snake in the grass." Also, we don't want to overlook good candidates we haven't heard about simply because they didn't have as much money to spend on advertising as their opponents.

I suggest you consider becoming the contact person for your church for one or more issue advocacy groups. This can be done informally or formally depending on the comfort level your church may have with the political world. I'm in no way suggesting deception. I'm saying that you can informally let others know of your involvement and ask them if they want any information prior to elections. In one sense this informal relationship may be better for your church. Your involvement will simply be that of an individual member rather than an official arm of the church's ministry.

My preference, of course is for every church to embrace our responsibility to be involved in what happens in our government and have a ministry of social concerns or of governmental affairs, or whatever title you may wish to give it. **It is still perfectly legal if it remains focused on issues rather than candidates and political parties.**

Let me emphasize what I mean here. **No church should EVER, I mean EVER, allow itself to be used as a political pawn by a candidate or party.** If we give in to that kind of pressure, we will lose our moral authority and Biblical witness. We will compromise our faith for political expediency. I saw this tension when I worked for the Christian Coalition back in the early 1990s. When Christians began to get involved and added life and fire to the political process, the political parties, especially the Republican Party attempted to subordinate the movement to Party leadership. In other words, the Party expected our members to support all of their candidates as loyal Republicans, even those whom we disagreed with on the issues. That was a recipe for disaster. Those who compromised and followed the rank and file lost their Christian distinctiveness. Those who refused were cast out of the Party and labeled disloyal.

I saw this again in 1994 with the Pennsylvania election for Governor. The establishment Republicans wanted to anoint Tom Ridge as their choice. Those in Christian political circles rebelled because Ridge was a pro-abort. Many arguments ensued across the state when Christians refused to toe the party line. In 1996 the PA Republican leadership instigated a state-wide purge of all the "religious fanatics" from the party. The state is just now starting to recover from this purge via the influence of the Tea Party Movement. But, this purge gave us eight years of the economically and ethically bankrupt Ed Rendell regime.

My point is this – we need to be greater than party politics in the church. For decades the urban black church has been a pawn of the Democrat Party. Thousands of sincere Christians are told to support candidates that take positions clearly in opposition to our faith and Biblical teachings. What has the result been? The conditions in many of our major cities remains blighted and the Democrat politicians have been entrenched there for decades. The "devil's bargain" that many of these churches have made has directly led to the ongoing misery and reduced quality of life for far too many good, decent, and sincere fellow Christians.

We, as the church, need to speak to the culture, not allow the ambitions of self-centered politicians to control what we say. We need to be free to proclaim God's Truth as it applies to the world of government. We need to, in some cases, "put the fear of God" back into politicians who believe they can say or do anything they want without fear of it costing them their highly-paid jobs.

If it is possible, suggest to those in your church's leadership the need for a committee or a group to deal with the important moral and social issues of the day, especially how they tie in to politics and elections. All of the members of the church should be informed as to what's going on in society. This is a basic step. **Knowledge is power.** A group of like-minded people in each church can do wonders to inform the whole congregation as to what is happening.

Second and third steps for this group to take are to keep people engaged and to train people how to participate. Issues don't go away after elections. Far too many people in government believe they can get away with doing things in Washington or in state capitols that will go unnoticed by most people. This has been all too true in the past especially given our slanted and incompetent media. Our people in churches need to know what is going on in local town council chambers, state capitols, and in Washington before the need arises to stop bad laws that have been enacted without our knowledge. Our people need to know in advance what issues will be coming before our elected representatives before they vote. Then, our people can make their voices heard very clearly and loudly. We will talk more about how to be most effective about that in a later chapter.   That is part of the basic training needed for our church folk. Our goal needs to be to have a church filled with citizens who fully participate in our nation's present and future governance.

Community Issues Advocacy:

If you find that your interest level is more intense and you have more time to commit to the issues that you feel passionate about, another option is to get involved with or start a group in your community. Perhaps you could begin a gun rights' group. Perhaps you could join a local pro-life group. Maybe you could organize people interested in seeing school choice become a reality. By working through a community group, your influence may be more effective and wide-spread than if you only work within your church.

For a number of years I was involved, and later served as president, of our county level pro-life group. We were affiliated with the National Right to Life Committee. It was strictly a volunteer organization, but we were influential in raising awareness about abortion. We got materials into many of the churches in our county. We held candidate forums. We distributed voter guides. We held rallies. We were part of the early Life Chain events. We also supported our local crisis pregnancy organizations. Both reporters and politicians would contact us with questions and to assure us of their pro-life stances. It was a great way to influence many people in our county. I worked with many dedicated people from many different occupations and churches. We were ecumenical and crossed many socio-economic categories.

It was a great experience for me. It also prepared me for an even greater role in attempting to shape culture. From there, I got involved with the Christian Coalition. This was a movement in the early 1990s of Christians seeking to educate and inform people about a broad range of social issues. I was still very pro-life, as they were, but I also was in a position to speak about other issues. I remember fighting battles over school choice, outcomes-based education, expansion of abortion clinics, and controlling the increase of obscenity. We also dealt with economic issues, term limits, and freedom of religion battles.

My point is – this level of involvement can be a great ministry for someone who has the time to put into it. It is desperately needed. **All too often Christians are seeking for someone to tell them the truth about issues and candidates.** If you get involved at this level, you could become that resource that your community looks to in times when they need answers. If nothing else, you can become a strong voice of witness for God's truth on one or more of the great issues of our day.

Lobbying:

This involvement with issues can be taken to a higher level than that of a busy volunteer. At some point, you might be able to become a lobbyist for your cause. It is true that we hear quite a bit of negative press about lobbyists today, much of it earned. However, every major issue, cause, and interest group has lobbyists in state capitols and in Washington. Many are ethical and passionate. Some are downright slimy and fraudulent. Obviously, our goal is to give our cause a good name and face.

This might be an option for you if you have the experience, expertise, and training to do it well. Your goal, as a lobbyist, is to convince your target politicians to vote for as many bills that agree with your position as possible. That isn't always easy, especially at the national level. Congressmen and Senators are bombarded by special interests all the time. The most skilled politicians know how to make everyone feel like they will get everything they want of them. Obviously, that doesn't happen. But, it is a dance that goes on all the time.

For us, our goal is to be honest and persuasive without compromising our faith. In fact, it will be a breath of fresh air for most politicians to know that we aren't there to "horse trade." Ronald Reagan once said that it might not always be possible to make some politicians see the light, but it is possible to make them feel the heat! A good lobbyist can convey to a politician that voting a certain way is not only ethical, but will also make the majority of people in their district happy.

Someday there may be lobbyist reform in government, but until that day comes, it behooves us to make sure our voices are heard by those in office. Being a professional ethical lobbyist can be a real and powerful ministry to shape this nation. It can be a calling for the right person.

Politics

The third category we wish to discuss here is that of political involvement. In this area, there are differing levels of commitment and different categories of jobs to do. The simplest way to break them down is in two categories: **elections' officials** and **party politics**.

Elections' Officials

Quite a bit of the voting fraud we have seen has resulted from incompetent or dishonest elections' officials not doing their jobs properly. Getting involved with your local elections' operation is one way to change that. In every voting location (usually called a precinct), there are a number of people who run the operation. Their title names may vary from state to state, but essentially they are a judge of elections, majority (party) inspector, minority (party) inspector, clerk, and constable. Each has a specific job to do to insure voting goes smoothly and honestly. These are usually paid positions. The pay isn't great, but it only requires a few days-worth of work each year. If we want to insure that our local election precinct is totally ethical in how elections are conducted, then these might be good opportunities for you. In order to serve in these positions, you need to run for the job. Usually, these offices are up for election during the years of local and county elections – generally the odd-year elections. Federal and many state elections are held in even years.

Above the local level are county level elections' officials. These people supervise voting operations within a county and are usually employed by an election bureau. At that level, more responsibility is required. It is also the place where greater fraud occurs. I can remember a director of our county election bureau being arrested and convicted back in the early 1990s for fixing a local election for a friend of his. The ballots were returned honestly to the election bureau, but he used his position of leadership to change the numbers. He has since served a jail term for his actions.

Working at the county level could mean everything from actually tabulating votes from the various precincts to certifying winners of elections. It also would include processing voter registration forms, compiling "street lists" of registered voters, and dealing with candidate petitions and ballot creation. The same type of work is done by state-level elections' workers.

These are vitally important jobs even if they don't often get much publicity. Perhaps you can remember the spectacle of elections' officials in Florida back in 2000 looking at stacks of paper ballots with "hanging chads" trying to sort out the mess of the 2000 Presidential election. The whole race came down to who actually won the state of Florida. The winner would be the next President. The first and second time the votes were counted, George W. Bush won by a few hundred votes. But, the Democrats had much to lose, so they kept getting judicial authority from Florida's Democrat-controlled Supreme Court to keep re-counting ballots. They would have kept on doing it until they "found" Al Gore enough votes if the U. S. Supreme Court didn't stop them a few weeks after the election was over.

This past political circus illustrates my point about needing good, honest, competent elections' officials at all levels very well. It is a great place for Christians to make a real difference. If, because we are honest people, ballots are secure and voter fraud is minimized, then we will have a greater system for electing leaders than we now possess. Every close election will raise questions. And, yes, every close election lends itself to voter fraud. That's because voter fraud has to be hidden to work. If it is blatant and obvious, the cowards who engage in it will not chance exposure. They will only work to add a few votes here and there. If we can stop that, then the percentage of dead people voting in places like Philadelphia and Chicago will decline sharply!

Party Politics

Party politics means volunteering or working for the political party of your choice. This also has many levels of involvement and commitments. Most of these positions are voluntary; a few are paid. Working for the political party of your choice can yield great results. You will be working directly to get people elected to government at all levels. This is very important in guiding the direction our country will go.

However, there is one drawback to working for a political party that must be discussed before we talk about the particulars of political party involvement. Those who are deeply committed to their party will expect the same level of commitment and loyalty from anyone else who works for the party. The potential problem for the Christian who gets involved with a political party is the issue of supporting party candidates with positions opposite our own. A political party worker who is a

Christian will be confronted with this dilemma. If the party endorses a candidate who is a pro-abort, they may not care if we are pro-life. They will expect all of the rank and file to work hard for that candidate. The same may be true of other candidates holding positions we disagree with.

So, what do we do? Do we compromise our faith in order to be loyal party supporters? Do we stand strong in our faith and risk alienating the party to whom we belong and have made commitments to support? This is a drawback of being involved in party politics. Obviously, **we Christians should never compromise our faith to satisfy some political agenda**. But, if we want to be a part of political parties we must find a way to show support for the party without compromising our faith. Some Christians may not want to face this choice. For others, they may seek a way to be both faithful to God and loyal to their party. It is possible in some instances to achieve both. If you are a party member who has a reasonable party chairman at your local level, he/she may recognize both your convictions and the positive contribution you make to the party. If that is the case, the party chairman will place you in a position to put your time into supporting those candidates you believe in supporting. If you have a political hack for a party chairman, he/she may demand a test of loyalty from you by seeking to get your support for someone you can't. In that case, your future in the party is going to be limited until the chairman is replaced by someone who can see the big picture.

I dealt with this back in 1994. I was involved with my party at a lower level. The party, from the state-level down, was pushing a pro-abort for governor. It was assumed that I would come out and support him as well. When asked about it I explained to everyone that the governor candidate had much of the rest of the party to work for him. I was going to put my time in working for the U.S. Senate candidate who was also running. He was a solid pro-life conservative. I'm sure there were those in the party who were angry with me, but they couldn't deny that I had worked hard for a candidate of their party, just not in the race they wanted. My faith was not compromised. I also was not disloyal to the party. By the way, the opponent of the governor candidate was also a pro-abort, so I had no choice to make about support for either side. I voted for neither.

My point is this: we need to decide if party politics is for us. We will be faced with both great opportunities and great moral choices if we get involved. None of the major political parties is "pure" in the sense we would be thinking. We can work outside the system to make changes to it, or we can work inside a flawed system to make changes from within. Ask God what He is calling you to do. He will give you the grace and peace regardless of which choice you make. There certainly is plenty of work to be done both outside of and within political parties.

For our discussion here, let's assume you have decided to get involved with a political party. What opportunities are there for service? Let's start at the bottom and work our way up.

Local Committee

A local or precinct committee person is responsible for getting votes in elections for the candidates of the party in that election. This is the basic unit of a political party. **This is the "grassroots" of politics.** If you serve as a precinct committee person, your first job is to get as many of your neighbors registered in your party as you can. Next, your job is to get information to them about the candidates running in the next election. Finally, your job is to encourage, urge, and drag (if necessary) them to the polls to vote on Election Day. To become a local committee person, you also have to be elected – usually during the same odd-year elections mentioned previously. An exception to this might be an appointment by a county party chairman if your local precinct committee position is vacant.

A second, but important responsibility of the precinct committee person is membership in the county political party. You will have to attend party meetings and gatherings. Often these are pep rallies and fund-raisers for candidates. But they are also meetings to decide strategy and endorsements of candidates. These meetings can become contentious if there are two or more candidates of your party seeking the same office. That means a contested Primary Election. These meetings are notorious for their "horse-trading" and "back-room dealing." Many in party leadership want to determine who the General Election candidates get to be, not trust the results of a Primary Election. If the party endorses one candidate over another, that means that candidate will have the party's official backing. The results of endorsement include party money, party workers, and party publicity. All of these are huge advantages to have in a Primary Election.

I know this sounds like pretty boring stuff, but here is where the real power lies in any political party. If you get a large group of like-minded people to run in their local precinct committee person elections, you stand a good chance of having a power bloc in the party, if not the strength to take over the county party outright! You want to be a voice in which the candidates are that run for county-wide offices. This is an opportunity to make sure you are helping to start the political careers of honest and competent people and blocking the potential careers of more corrupt, greedy politicians. This also has a pyramid effect to the state and national level as well.

State Committee

Those who serve at the State Committee level have a huge say in the direction a state may go. State Committee members are usually made up of elected officials in your county and a number of people who run for the office. Each state and county and party has their specific rules about who gets to be a State Committee person. Generally, the position entails attending state party conventions and meetings a few times a year. State Committee members vote on endorsements of state-wide candidates. This includes state-level offices like Governor and Attorney General. It also includes national offices like U.S. Senator and possibly U. S. House members.

It is an opportunity to influence the direction a whole state moves politically. It is also an opportunity to groom and train future state and national leaders. In addition, State Committee members are active in their local county's politics; generally having an influential voice in what a county-level political party does. State Committee members are often asked to recruit candidates for office. They are asked to help in fund-raising efforts for the party and its candidates. They are often interviewed when issues arise involving their political party.

Being a member of a party's State Committee is a busy volunteer job. It can have great results for the right person. It is also a position of power that the professional politicians covet. The establishment politicians tend to guard the positions closely. They want to control what a state party does. They also want to be sure that there are no surprises within the party. The issues already discussed concerning working within a political party certainly apply here to the State Committee position.

National Committee

For all practical purposes, to serve as a National Committee person for a party means that you are wealthy and can commit almost full-time effort to the advancement of your party. Fund-raising is a large part of what you will be doing. You will also be traveling throughout the country as well. Usually National Committee people are appointed by the state party. State-wide elected officials are generally given membership to the national party leadership. Others may be appointed by the leadership of the state committees. Generally those appointments have to be approved by the national party leadership.

In other words, this is not the position of the average politically active person. That is not to say that you couldn't work your way to that point if the Lord was leading you in that direction. Certainly the national parties could use more good, honest, moral people leading them. But, understand that few people can currently qualify for this level of party leadership.

National Convention Delegate

Every four years the national parties hold a national convention. This always coincides with the Presidential election. A way to participate in these conventions is to become a National Convention Delegate. This is a temporary position. You will only serve for the convention. Each state is allotted so many delegates to the convention; usually based on population. Some of the delegates are elected officials. But, it is possible to get elected to the position. Generally, this happens during the Primary Election the year of the Presidential election. Candidates are chosen from those on the ballot from the U.S. House District in which they live.

The National Convention Delegate has two basic functions. **First, the delegates cast their votes for the candidate they are pledged to support.** The candidate that gets over the minimum number of delegates' votes needed at the convention becomes the Party's nominee for President. In recent years this task was a bit mundane as one candidate from each party had more than enough delegates coming in to the convention to guarantee the nomination. The result was that the conventions became a huge, several-day pep rally to get their nominee elected in the fall.

But, in the past, conventions were held where no one candidate had enough votes for the nomination. Each party sets its own rules, but generally the delegates were pledged to vote for a specific candidate only on the first ballot. After they cast that vote, if there was no clear winner, they were free to vote for whomever they wished on the following ballots. This led to some interesting results at political conventions with some nominees emerging only after days and days and several votes taken.

If any convention doesn't know who the winner will be coming in, then being a National Convention Delegate takes on an extra importance. Groups and factions will form and coalitions of delegates will band together to come up with enough votes to get their candidate "over the top." Talk about "horse-trading", "back-room deals", and political compromises! But, if there are enough good, godly delegates there, the best candidate will emerge. The problem is that when a candidate for National Convention Delegate has to register a petition to get on a Primary ballot, there is no way of knowing whether the convention will be cut and dried or filled with intrigue.

A second important job, though not often discussed in the press, **which National Convention Delegates do is come up with a national party platform**. This is a series of statements of beliefs that the party holds. These various topics, called "planks", define a political party. This is where it is critical to have good people involved in the process. Will your party be known as a pro-life party? Will they be known as the party of lower taxes? Will they be the party of homosexual marriage? All of these issues and more will be determined by what is written in the party platform. And, since the party platform is written and voted on by the delegates, being there is of great importance.

Both of these tasks make being a National Convention Delegate an important job to do. You could literally be choosing the next President of the United States as well as defining what your party stands for on all of the important issues of the day.

Campaigns

One other category of political involvement we haven't discussed yet is being involved in specific campaigns for office. This is active political involvement, but not ongoing party politics. No one gets elected to office without the help of others. The higher the office, the larger the army of volunteers and staff needed to wage a successful campaign. Let's look at what opportunities are available for you if you want to get involved with this aspect of politics.

Campaign Volunteer

The most common position of any campaign is that of volunteer. Every political campaign has quite a bit of diversified work that needs to be done to get the candidate's message out and his/her supporters to the polls on Election Day. This takes a large group of volunteers to be successful. Following is a partial list of activities that campaign volunteers do in any successful campaign:

Answering phones	Distributing literature
Placing yard signs	Stuffing envelopes
Monitoring media	Catering
Handing out literature at the polls	
Decorating	
Setting up/tearing down event venues	

In addition to these, often volunteers also assist in maintaining social media, setting up speaking engagements, act as poll watchers, deliver materials to activists, and do issues and opposition research.

Being a volunteer is a great way to directly help a candidate you believe in. As a volunteer, you can give whatever time you have to give. You can do the jobs you prefer to do, or have the specific abilities to do. And, you can feel a part of a team that makes things happen in your state capitol or in Washington. It also means your commitment is expected in campaign season, but you won't have to give any time between elections. Campaigns are always looking for competent, committed volunteers. We, Christians, understand about serving. This is a great opportunity to serve in this area of our nation. If we can get our candidates elected, we can feel a satisfaction that we are making a real difference.

Campaign Staff

At the level above volunteer is that of Campaign Staff. This is a paid position within a campaign. If you are qualified to hold one of these positions, it means you are a trusted member of your candidate's campaign leadership team. You will be deeply involved with the campaign. It generally means many long hours; especially as the election nears. You will be supervising the group of volunteers that are helping with your component of the campaign. The job you do, good or bad, could make or break your candidate.

Campaign staff does everything from writing position papers of the candidates to securing locations for speaking events. They monitor social media and websites. They deal with the press. Sometimes they keep an otherwise exhausted candidate going. It is a grueling, often frustrating job that can be filled with satisfaction. Getting your candidate elected means a great victory for your skills as well as their attractiveness to voters.

Very often, Campaign Staff become permanent staff of the candidate when they get elected. If you are competent and loyal, you might find yourself with your own office in your state capitol or in Washington right next to your boss's! Or, you might be running one of the candidate's local offices back home – dealing with constituents on a daily basis.

In either case, being on a campaign staff or an elected official's staff, you will be doing politics and government full time. It must be your passion to do it well. It could be a great ministry for the right person. Most elected officials look to their staff for advice and ideas on the various issues. You would be in such a place of trust at that point.

Running for Office

The final step of political involvement is running for office. You are stepping out of the advocacy and support role now and aspiring to a leadership role in our government. Whether we are speaking about town council or President of the United States, or any other position in between, to serve in government is just as much a calling as serving in the ministry is. **Our governments will succeed or fail depending on the quality of the men and women who occupy the offices of power.** We have all seen this. Solomon told us this in Proverbs 29:2

> **"When the righteous increase, the people rejoice,**
> **But when a wicked man rules, people groan."** (NASB)

Choosing to run for office is a decision never to be taken lightly. As stated previously, Paul calls rulers "ministers of God" and "servants of God" in Romans 13:4-6. We must see ourselves in this light if we choose to run for office. The world is filled with the power-hungry and corrupt who will seek to fill these positions for their own personal reasons. We must be different. To serve in government is to serve God first, the people second, and our own needs last. Without this commitment, we will fail.

God wants to raise up generations of good leaders. From among us people must arise and take on the responsibility of serving at all levels of government if we are to survive as a nation. The cost may be great. The road may be long. But, the satisfaction of knowing we were faithful to God and promoted freedom and the general welfare of society is great for those who are called.

To do this, our families, our friends, and our churches must be behind us in support. The temptations, assaults, and the frustrations can be great at times for those in authority. Anyone who thinks they can serve well without daily reliance on the Lord is a fool. It takes much prayer and counsel from those we trust to help us decide if it is the right thing to do. And, when we have made our minds up to take on this mantle of authority, we must go forth boldly, trusting God for the outcome.

From a practical point of view, if you have never participated in the political arena before, it's best to work your way up through the ranks, learning as you go. The unknown person, who suddenly shows up at church and announces God told him to run for President, probably has some serious spiritual, if not psychological problems. But, the person from your community who shows up at church and asks your opinion as to whether they should run for school board or town council is probably someone God is preparing for greater things.

God will make it plain to you if He is calling you to do this vital task. It may be for just a time, or it may be the beginning of a life-long career. It may even take a few defeats along the way before you are ultimately successful. But, if you feel the passion to serve building within you; and you have the skills and abilities needed to do the job well; and you feel God's Presence guiding you, then you should seriously consider becoming a "minister of God for good", as Paul so aptly put it.

Chapter 7: What Can My Church Do?

The Church, the Body of Christ in the world, has a definite role to play in the direction our culture moves. Despite what today's secular, self-anointed "experts" might tell us, we do have a right; no, in fact, a responsibility to have our voices heard in the debate about how we as a society will live. That is a non-negotiable truth we must fight to the death to defend. Without the influence of the Christian Church today, our culture has absolutely no hope. This nation and the world as a whole would descend into darkness in a matter of just a couple of years without our influence.

So, what can each of our local churches do in this battle for our culture? The simple answer is – **a whole lot more than we may think!** We are the people of God! We have the truth in our hearts and on our lips. Our influence in the world cannot simply be from behind church walls. It is true that Jesus commissioned us to go into all the world to preach the Gospel. But, He also told us to be salt and light in the world as well. In fact, many of the problems we face today are either directly or indirectly linked to the Church's failure to be salt and light in our culture over the past 50 or so years.

When God's people seek to include God's truth in every area of our culture, everyone benefits; believers and non-believers alike. When we withdraw and allow secular visions of societal utopia to carry the day, the whole of society crumbles. Let's use one historical comparison. During the Great Depression of the 1930s, the unemployment rate was close to 25%. There was no welfare state. There was no government safety net of any kind. With those desperate conditions, one might think the crime rates went through the roof. But, that is not the case. You see, the nation still openly practiced the Christian faith. Most families were intact. Very, very few had a sense of entitlement from the government or from those who were wealthy. As a result, families drew closer together. They sacrificed together. They shared resources as best they could. Churches did more to help the poor than ever before.

Historians will debate the relative worth of FDR's New Deal program. But, the truth is that **it was the strength of the American Church and family that carried people through the Great Depression and World War II**. The age of American greatness that the late 1940s, 1950s, and 1960s brought can be directly tied to the character of the people who used faith to fight the long odds of the Depression and the War. Poverty and privation did not lead to societal breakdown. It made people stronger. It made families stronger. It made communities stronger.

Let's contrast that to the minor economic downturns we have seen over the past 40 years. In that time, we have seen the nuclear family all but destroyed. God has been removed from much of public life. The schools and universities are atheist strongholds. Decency and honorable behavior are now only joked about. And, the new "sacrament" of the secularists is tolerance - which is simply code for allowing anyone to do anything they want with absolutely no moral judgments whatsoever!   The Great Society programs, started by LBJ in the mid-1960s have transferred over 16 trillion dollars of wealth from one group to another in this nation. Yet, despite that massive effort, we still have poverty in this country. But, we can hardly call the poverty of today equal with that of the Great Depression. This nation has the richest poor people in the world.

However, our jails are full. Child abuse is rampant. We have murdered over 55 million children because of "choice." Our schools turn out young people who can't compete internationally. The tax burden is growing beyond 50% total for most households. Millions of promising young lives have been lost to totally preventable social diseases. The culture has coarsened. Age is no longer revered. Euthanasia advocates have gained a foothold here. We are well on our way to collapse economically due to massive government and personal debt.

What is the reaction to all of this by the elitist social engineers and professional politicians? We need far more of the same! We need to spend more and more on social programs that destroy worth and responsibility. We need to destroy the last remaining vestiges of morality, traditional families, and faith in God. Their recipe for disaster hasn't changed. They are just angry that it is taking so long to completely re-make America in their utopian Marxist image. Anyone who dares disagree with or criticize their plans and philosophy is ignorant, subversive, and a threat to the nation; at least that's what they would have the uninformed believe.

It is high time for us to stop the insanity! Only the Church can do this. We are the only ones left who have the commitment to the truth and the numbers to make real change in this society. We can no longer afford to remain silent. We can no longer be embarrassed to discuss "dirty politics" in our sanctuaries. We can no longer plead the same kind of ignorance the German folk did who lived near the concentration camps. We will be held accountable if we don't do our best to reverse the course before our nation plunges off the precipice of history. We cannot stand one day before God and shrug our shoulders at the great tragedy of our time.

So, let's get started! First of all, let me make clear that our involvement is not just a part of any political party or candidacy. **The Church is far greater than politics and politicians**. We will never subjugate our mission to anyone on earth; especially not to government experts or demagogues intent on replacing God with their own agenda. That's not to say we are anarchists. As we previously stated, we believe in government as an instrument of God for good in society. **We don't want "no" government. We want "good" government. We will settle for nothing less**. We will work as hard as we have to to make that dream a reality. If we can unite and maintain our motivation, no power on earth will be able to stop us from restoring freedom and opportunity to this land. And, the powers of Hell will not be able to stop us from restoring the truth of God's love for all of His people into every area of culture.

That is not to say that we want to devolve the Church into little more than a social movement of sorts. That's what happened to the theologically liberal mainline churches. That's also why their numbers are shrinking at steady and alarming rates. They have abandoned Biblical truth for religious socialist liberation theology and whatever the latest sophomoric sociology theories dictate. No, we don't ever want to become like them. We will maintain our faithfulness to God's Word. But, engaging the culture and the government while still being true to the Word is easily doable. We don't want the Church to run the government. And, we certainly don't want the government to dictate to the Church. We've seen how miserably both scenarios have failed in history. But, we need to have both a healthy Church and a healthy government if our society, and all of its people, are to reach their potential. **If either institution fails, so will our nation**.

What should our churches look like if we want to maximize our efforts in this area? Let's take a closer look. Our pews are filled with informed voting citizens who know how to cut through the political smokescreens erected by the professional "spin merchants." We have committees set up to monitor both legislatures and legislative issues in an effort to provide solid current information for the congregation as a whole. We have tables and bulletin boards set up in hallways with the latest doings on all of the major issues. We have links on our websites to Christian news organizations providing information we can trust to be accurate and unbiased. Every member has a complete listing of their elected representatives conveniently located near their telephones and computers at home.

We have members handing out non-partisan voters' guides before every election. We sponsor candidate forums before each election where all candidates are invited to attend and share their views. We have a chain of communication set up so that people can be notified at a moment's notice of pending legislation. We have people sitting in the pews who are members of the local schools boards, the town councils, and who are active in the political parties of their choices.

We teach classes in our Christian education departments about the institution of government from a Biblical perspective. Our Christian schools teach civics and the Constitution. They also teach the history of American Exceptionalism and basic free-market economic theory.

And, we are probably being picketed by left-wing interest groups upset that we are getting the truth out about their agenda.

Sounds like a very tall order? Not really. We can grow our churches in these areas with a bit of vision, commitment, and effort on our part. Let's take a look at how to achieve these ideas just mentioned. (By the way, I'm sure there are more things that can and are being done than I've listed.) For the sake of our discussion, let's assume your church is currently doing nothing. Where do you start? **First and foremost, you pray**. You seek out other like-minded folk in your church and start gathering together to pray. Pray for your church. Pray for the nation. Pray for those in leadership in government. Pray for people's eyes to be opened. Pray for God's guidance as to what will best work in your church. And, pray for your leadership (pastor and church board) to be open to starting these types of ministries.

The second phase of this is to give your prayers "feet." Invite others from your church to join your prayer group. **Grow the prayer group into a prayer and discussion group**. For that, you may wish to use a number of resources. Maybe you would like to discuss chapters in this book. Maybe you would get materials from *Wallbuilders* (Such as *America's Godly Heritage*, *The American Heritage Series*, and others) to present and discuss.

After people are more educated about the Bible and government and our Christian American heritage, you can see which issues people would like to find more out about. People can begin to do research about various issues and share what they've learned with the group. Other folks may want to research your various government representatives. They can find out who they are and what their views and voting records are. No one needs to re-invent the wheel here. Quite a bit of this information is already out there. They just need to tap into it.

When your group is praying for the nation, your church, your community, and those in authority; and when your group has a good grasp of the issues and the political landscape; then you may be ready to approach your church leadership to begin a ministry in your church. Speak to the pastor and the church board about your interest and ideas. Please always reassure them that your efforts will be non-partisan and perfectly legal for churches. Assuming they are in agreement, you are ready to begin making your church a force for societal change!

The first place to start is with education. Since we Christians need to have a Biblical foundation for everything we do, starting with a Bible Study on the Bible and government may be the best initial effort on your part. It's not about issues or elections at this point. It's about what God wants His people to do in supporting the kind of government He has ordained. Having a church full of people who understand what God says about what government will be is a great start to change a community for the better. A secondary study connected to this is to describe the great amount of Christian influence the founding of this nation has had. Most people, especially those with public school educations, have no idea just how much Christianity is inculcated within America's very fiber. ***Wallbuilders* is a great resource for this kind of info. Books by William Federer, Peter Marshall, and others are also helpful.**

After people become informed, the next logical step is providing opportunities for involvement. Again, this can be first done without issues or politics being at the forefront. Start by having non-partisan voter registration drives in your church. Obtain voter registration forms from the local election bureau or other public facilities such as post offices and libraries. Have a voter registration Sunday at your church. Provide volunteers to help people fill out the forms after a worship service. Remember, do not pressure anyone. And, do not tell anyone which political party to register with. It is perfectly permissible to have the national party platforms available to people so they can see which party best fits their views. These are usually available online from the national party websites.

When you have a church with a large majority of registered voters, two subsequent steps are indicated. First, for those who have never voted before, you may need to give a brief class on voting procedure. No one wants to appear foolish in public. By explaining the voting procedures to them, you take away fear and increase participation. Another service you can provide is to request someone from the election bureau to come to your church and show how to use voting machines. This is important, especially for older new voters, who may feel intimidated by the technology. I remember the first time I took my mother to vote after the county had installed new electronic voting machines. I had to walk her through the whole procedure. Even though she was someone who had voted via paper ballot her whole life, it was very intimidating.

I have also found that some people may be embarrassed that they aren't registered to vote. An "out" I have used in this case is to explain to people that their voter registration may have expired if they haven't voted in a few elections. Every state is different, so you may need to fill in the blank as to how long a period of time elapses before your state removes inactive voters from the registration rolls. This way, they can feel at ease to register without having to disclose that they have never voted before.

The natural second step is to provide candidate information. When an election is looming, people will always want to know who to vote for. That will be an opportunity to provide voter guides for your church. Again, the role of any church committee is to provide non-partisan voter information, not to tell people who to vote for. Many organizations create voters' guides before elections. If your committee taps into their resources, you don't have to start from scratch. Just be sure that the organizations' information contained on the guides is accurate. The last thing you want to do is put out information that is false or incomplete. That is not to say that some politicians won't resent their voting records being exposed to the public. Some may howl that they are unfairly being targeted by an organization whose issues they disagree with or have voted against. But, that doesn't matter. Our job is to get the truth out there and let the chips fall where they may.

I will never forget the reaction I got from many during the 1992 Presidential Election. Many conservatives jumped on the Ross Perot bandwagon. They thought he was a breath of fresh air and would change things for the better. But, when it was revealed that Perot was pro-abortion, believed in special rights for homosexuals, and had made most of his money through government contracts processing bureaucratic paperwork, their views on him changed radically. People were shocked. Some didn't believe me. Unfortunately, the message didn't get out to enough voters until after the election. Many who voted for him had quite a bit of "buyers' remorse" after the fact!

My point is that **we need to put good information into the hands of our people and then trust them to make the right choices when they vote**. We do not want to become just like the radical left in this country that treats their constituents like children. We do not want to deceive anyone. And, we certainly never ever want to engage in the same kind of voter fraud that has become accepted practice in their political camps. When all of our people are informed voting citizens, we will become a powerful force to be reckoned with.

For local elections, such as school boards, town councils, mayoral races, and county-wide elections, we may need to produce our own voters' guides. If there is no local organization following those in local government, you may have to put that work in yourselves. Questionnaires can be produced and distributed by your committee for all elected offices you want to feature in your guides. Just be sure to survey all candidates running for the offices you choose to report about. You do not want to be accused of being biased. All of the candidates may not respond to your questionnaires, but you can indicate a non-response on your guides.

One other piece of advice for creating your local guides – try to keep your candidate questionnaire questions relevant to issues they are, or will be dealing with in their offices. It may be of interest for some people to know where your mayoral candidates stand on the issue of Iran getting nukes, but it is doubtful a town mayor will ever have to make a decision based on that issue. Stick to what they will be dealing with. People need to know if the mayor will push for an increase in garbage collection fees. People need to know where a school board member stands on teacher tenure vs. merit pay increases. People need to know whether or not a town council member would vote to grant a zoning variance to allow an adult club in your town. Relevance is what is most important for these local guides.

A further step your church can take prior to elections is to host a candidates' forum. This is an excellent opportunity for your members to hear and meet those running for office that they will soon need to consider voting for or against. This is especially true for local elections. What candidate for mayor would not come to candidates' forum at a church in the town in which they are running? You may also be able to attract candidates for state or federal offices if your forums become well-attended and publicized. Again, these are excellent opportunities for voters to meet the candidates. This is also an excellent opportunity to showcase your church to the community. Of course, you want to invite the public to attend. But, just remember to keep it non-partisan.

Invite all of the candidates. Give each equal time. But, allow the audience to ask what questions they will. There is no need to attempt to censor questions because they don't necessarily represent the church's position or views. Also, if your event is potentially very successful, expect the press to be there. That's fine; just don't allow yourself to be cornered by a reporter into declaring support for certain candidates by the church. Remember, the goal is getting information to the voters, nothing more. Our side trusts our people to vote consistent with their consciences and beliefs.

If your church becomes comfortable with this level of involvement, the next step is to keep members informed on issues pending in the legislatures. **Timely communications from large numbers of people can affect the success or failure of most legislation**. We want our people to know what's going on and when so they can effectively express their opinions to those they have elected to represent them. Legislative alerts can be posted on a bulletin board where people can see them and respond as they feel led. A monthly flier can be created to inform people what is coming up in the near future of the state and federal law-making bodies. Phone numbers, email addresses, social media site addresses, and mailing addresses can be posted for all of the legislators serving your congregation. Booklets or info sheets containing these addresses and phone numbers can be distributed to each member. Relevant news articles can also be posted and distributed as appropriate.

The bottom-line goal with this effort is to make sure our people know what is going on at all levels of government and providing them an opportunity to express their opinions about such matters as they desire. More than one unscrupulous politician has reformed his ways when he began to realize that there were people watching his every legislative move! Honest, decent, public servants also relish the thought that people are seeing the good they are doing in their offices.

These are just a few of the efforts churches can make to influence our government today. All are perfectly legal. None will diminish the Church's mission to reach out to the lost for Christ. People will begin to thank you for your hard work and effort for their sake. Remember, most people don't have the time to keep up on all of this stuff. If they have trusted sources to turn to in getting the information they need, they will be very grateful. They will also participate at a much higher level.

So, are you ready to begin to take your church's "salt" and "light" into the realm of American government? Just remember, to build and maintain your efforts, the secret of on-going success is prayer, prayer, prayer! **If we seek to honor the Lord in all we do, He will bless us richly!** God will use His people to proclaim His truth. His truth extends into the government arena as well as all the rest of the world. Remember the Psalmist's words:

"The earth is the Lord's and all it contains." (Ps. 24:1 NASB)

Chapter 8: Influencing Issues and Legislation

It has been said that most politicians are motivated by either fear or money. Since we are honest people who don't bribe those in government to get what we want, that leaves fear as a tactic for us to employ. I should qualify my previous statements. Jaded, cynical politicians are motivated by fear and money. Unfortunately for us, we may be dealing with a large number of these types of politicians in our neck of the woods. We all do know honest courageous government servants who are trying to do what is right. They are not the problem. However, given our current economic and moral crises in this nation, we have to assume we still have a majority of these, less than honorable men and women at the helms of leadership. Someday, if we are effective and stay engaged, we can change this reality, but for now it is what we are dealing with at the moment.

So, having said that, the question is, "How do we best put the 'fear of God' into those who represent us? How do we maximize our efforts to get good legislation passed and bad laws repealed?" To answer these questions, we must understand the dynamics of politics and government. Everyone who runs for office does so because they believe they can gain power and influence over the society and culture. Even people on our side realize, or they should realize, that in order to change things for the better, you have to have the authority to initiate the change. In other words, we also need to have political power to change the current status quo.

Power in and of itself is not the problem. As we stated previously, God ordained governments to wield power for the benefit of society. What is the problem is the gross misuse of power by those motivated by selfish greed and ambition. They are the ones destroying this nation. They are the ones who have become arrogant and out of touch with those whom they represent and the calling of their offices. It's a shame that it often boils down to this, but it is true.

It is also a truism that – **Arrogance Makes You Stupid!** I have seen this truth play out over and over again in the political world. Many a scandal-ridden politician has disappeared from view, still not realizing what the big deal was. You see, they get to positions of power, wealth, and authority and then they start to believe they are above the laws they have sworn to uphold. It also makes them out of touch with reality to some extent. Former governor of South Carolina, Mark Sanford, thought that he could just sneak off to South America to engage in an affair and no one would notice. Former U.S. Rep. Anthony Weiner thought that he could send pictures of his genitals to women on the internet and no one would find out. From our perspective, we say, "How could either of them have been so stupid?" But, the truism comes in to play. U.S. Rep. Charles Rangel evades paying thousands of dollars in taxes because of one of his homes in Central America and he acts astonished that the Congress officially reprimands him for his gross abuse of power. U.S. Treasury Secretary Tim Geithner cheats on his own taxes (yes, he does supervise the IRS) and blames it on his computer software. Again, these people are both arrogant and clueless. And, once again we "normal" people scratch our heads

So given this kind of cloistered elitist climate in politics among far too many, how do we influence what goes on? How does the "little guy" have a voice in all of this? To answer these questions, we must return to a few truisms; a few truisms that we must accept and practice. First of all, we must understand that – **Knowledge is Power!** That's right. The more we know about the political system, the workings of government, and the issues we are passionate about, the more power we will have to affect change. This may seem boring at times. It may seem like we don't have the time to re-learn basic civics. But, if we remain ignorant, we will always be at a disadvantage to those we oppose. The political left in this country are well versed in how the system works. They know how to manipulate public opinion and media. They know our weak spots and how to exploit them. And, since they generally have no morals, they will lie, cheat, steal, and worse to stay in power.

That is our first lesson in our quest for knowledge's power – **never underestimate the lengths our opponents will go to keep all they have seized from the American people**. Presidential candidate Herman Cain learned that lesson the hard way. I am certainly not suggesting that we stoop to the level of the left's depravity. We don't have to get down in the gutter with them to be successful. And, you can't use Satan's tactics to accomplish God's will. But, we must see our opponents clearly for who they are. It's like Ron Paul's "Pollyanna" view of Iran getting nukes. If he ever got into the Oval Office, only God would be left to help the nations of Europe, Israel, and the rest of the world! Being naïve will get us nowhere in the real world. This is a battle for the soul of our nation! The enemy will not stop unless it is forced to stop.

Second, we can't afford to have a fatalistic view of the future. It used to drive me crazy when I heard Christians say, "God will decide who the President should be." I think they thought that God would somehow supernaturally stuff the ballot boxes with enough votes for the right candidate if they only prayed. How silly and gullible! Edmund Burke's famous quote is relevant at this point – "The only thing necessary for the triumph of evil is for good men to do nothing." God gave us the blessing of self-rule. If we shun that blessing, we can lose it. Our non-participation has the same effect as working against freedom. **Sitting on the sidelines is no longer an option if we are to have a future**.

A second truism comes into play next – there is **Strength in Numbers!** We cannot do this task alone. We will be crushed if we try. We will make ourselves prime targets for the enemy if we try to go it alone. We need each other. We need to grow our ranks with people who mostly agree with us. We need to continue to educate those who are still ignorant of things. If we demand absolute agreement on every issue or absolute doctrinal purity by our members, we will fail. We need to seek out people that we have more in common with rather than look for the divisions. Yes, there will be times when we must separate ourselves from the group because of our principles. But, that doesn't mean we must cast out all of those who haven't evolved as far politically as we see ourselves.

Benjamin Franklin said it well immediately after those 56 world-changing Founding Fathers signed the Declaration of Independence – "We must all hang together, or assuredly we shall all hang separately." He understood squarely that the task that lay ahead of them was impossible with anything less that unity and mutual support for the cause of freedom. We are in the same boat today. If we don't coalesce, all will be lost. If we don't bring all who are potentially on our side into our ranks, we have no hope of winning.

I used the Franklin quote once, sadly, to no avail. Our group of conservatives had just made major inroads in our county's Republican party. The chairman was one of us. We had recently finished an election cycle where most of our candidates had won their elections for county offices. We were poised to overthrow the country club, establishment Republicans who had decimated the party with their abuse of power for decades. But, we reached a place where they decided to push back. They threatened to cause problems if we didn't support their move to install one of their own as party chairman – to replace our guy. They even suggested a state senator take the position. What we should have realized is just how tenuous their grip on power was. To have to resort to having the highest ranking elected Republican in the county take a giant step backwards to run the minutia of the party clearly showed their weakness. But, not everyone within our group could see the big picture.

A meeting was called with the members of our group and a State Rep. who had one foot in each world. He was conservative on the issues, but he craved the establishment's money and influence in order to keep his career alive. He came and spoke to us about the need to keep the party unified. For "the good of the party" our guy should step down. He should take a vice-chairmanship instead and keep the other side happy. After he left we talked. It was at this point I used the Franklin quote. I didn't realize, of course at the time, just how prophetic those words would be. Some within our group began to get cold feet. They were afraid that we couldn't see the "crisis" through and we would end up with nothing if we didn't heed the State Rep.'s advice.

The group fractured along three fissures. A group of those in office and those seeking future office were afraid their careers would come to nothing if we didn't go for the compromise. They thought we should live to fight another day and take the compromise now. A second group, who thought discord was distasteful, also wanted the compromise in order to restore their view of peace within the party. Finally, I was part of a smaller faction that wanted to reject the compromise, let the chips fall where they may, and push forward with our agenda, trusting the people of the county to rally to our side when they saw the good we were doing. Needless to say, I was out-voted. Our group decided to go for the compromise.

The end result was disaster. Our inroads so scared the establishment that they instituted a purge of the party over the next few years. Almost every one of our people that we got into public office was defeated in the next election. People who thought they would be chosen to run for office were shunned by the party leadership. Our chairman was relegated to second-class status in the party. And, our movement was effectively dead within four years. For the next decade, Democrats dominated county politics. The establishment Republicans had won the battle with us due to our false perception of reality and our divisions. But, they lost the war of governing the county.

I can't blame the establishment. They reacted like any dog would that was losing its bone. It was our fault. Just when we had the bone out of the dog's mouth, we gave it back to them! Because we didn't stand together, strong and united, all that we worked for fell apart. The State Rep. got some of what he wanted. When the state senator died in an accident, he managed to get elected to his office. But, when he ran for U.S. Rep., he got crushed by a mediocre Democrat. His losses were the biggest in our county since there was no strong Republican grass roots army to boost his chances. You see, they were all removed by the establishment.

It was just a few years ago that I bumped into the guy who was our chairman. He surprised me by remembering the meeting where I quoted Franklin. He said I turned out to be absolutely right in my prediction. It was sore solace considering what we lost. But, at least it proved the wisdom in what Franklin asserted.

My point is – **we must stay united or we will never win!** We are far stronger when we are unified than when we are divided. It reminds me of the Roman Legions. The armies of Rome conquered much of the known world because they fought as a strong unified force. Each man knew his task. He also knew he could count on those men on either side to protect his weaknesses. When they formed their famous "turtle" formations, they swept many a barbarian army right off the battle field. With the Lord at our heart, and united together, we can also be invincible in this battle for the soul of our culture!

OK, that said, where do we start to influence what happens at our state capitals and in Washington? We have discussed the first two components in the battle – information and unity. We must know what we are talking about and we must be unified in our efforts to bring about the changes we seek. The next step involves strategy. Holding mindless protests like the Occupy Wall Street Movement will accomplish next to nothing. Those mostly lazy college students would not have even been heard from had not the government unions and the media kept them pumped up.

So, how do we not make the same mistakes they did? How can we express our views in a way that those in power will, at best listen to our advice and, at worst, lose a lot of sleep worrying about their next election now that they know we are here. First, we need to work with groups already in existence who are working to foster change in the areas we want. Many of these advocacy groups have people on their staffs who know how the system works and how to frame the issues and the legislation in order to get it passed into law. We need to connect with them. If we agree with their views and their efforts, we must give them what support we can. We need to donate to their efforts. We need to distribute their literature. We need to volunteer to help get the message out. And, when necessary, we need to show up at their rallies so that our sheer numbers scare the bejeepers out of those in office!

Part of this means **we need to form coalitions to increase our numbers and influence**. Today's Democrat Party is a rag-tag group of political "odd-fellows." They are comprised of the labor unions, the environmental extremists, the homosexual lobby, the radical feminist abortionists, the academic elitists, Hollywood, a majority of African-Americans, and, of course, the trial lawyers. None of these groups really like each other, but they come together because they hate conservatives, Christians, and traditional families even more. They have been successful because they work together to get people into office that will further their ends.

We have tended to stay compartmentalized in our efforts. **We need to coalesce with those whom we share common goals**. We need pro-family folks to support the free market capitalists and the pro-lifers to support the pro-second amendment folks. We need conservative evangelicals to support traditional Catholics. We need the strong defense people to support the home-schoolers and everyone to support the traditional marriage people. I know there already is some overlap here, but we need to come together in greater and more diverse numbers. If we can unify and support each other, we can win most legislative battles and win most elections.

Another step we must take to influence legislation is to understand the legislative process. It takes quite a bit of work to get a law passed. That is true of both the state and federal levels. Unless it is some kind of emergency legislation, usually involving spending money, getting a bill turned into a law may take months or years. We may think that is very inefficient, but it is part of the plan our Founding Fathers gave us. They were looking to have a stable society, not one that would remake itself every time there was an election. They intentionally gave us representative democracy that would work slowly. By setting up both a federal system – with state and federal responsibilities, and a separation of powers with checks and balances, they hoped government would be somewhat self-regulating. Ultimately they left control in the hands of the people, however.

What we are seeing today, with the ever-increasing power of the federal government, is what results when citizens abrogate their responsibilities and interest groups vie for power to the detriment of the nation. It was never intended to be this way. It has happened largely because those in the legislative branch of government have been cowards to take on the tough issues. It is far easier for them to allow un-elected bureaucrats to create regulations or pass off issues to the appointed-for-life federal courts. Hence, *We The People*, have lost more and more control over those we appoint to serve us in government. This has led to discouragement and apathy on the part of far too many citizens of this Republic.

So, how do we change that? **We re-engage!** We learn the legislative system. We instruct those in office to take control of the agenda. We guide them as to what we want for our society. And, we refuse to accept excuses for failure! We need all elected officials to understand that their careers are in our hands. If they refuse to listen to us, they will have to find a new career right after the next election.

As I stated previously, this means we have to learn how things work when it comes to legislation. Let me give you a brief primer. (By the way, what I'm describing here is federal legislation. State-level legislation is similar, but some aspects may be different in your state.) Let's say you call Congressman "Smith" to tell him to make school choice a law of the land. If he is willing to listen, his first step is to offer a bill in Congress making school choice legal. (He may seek the aid of some of his fellow Congressmen as co-sponsors of the bill to aid its passage.) The bill is then assigned a number and referred to the relevant committees for further study. In this case it would probably be the Education Committee and possibly a few other secondary committees.

The bill will sit in the Education Committee until the chairman of the committee decides to deal with it. He can do nothing, order hearings, call for a vote to "table" it, or proceed to have a vote in the committee on the bill. A motion to "table" a bill is effectively killing it. It means it will sit in the committee without further action unless the committee chooses to deal with it at some future date. Hearings on the bill can also be a way to promote or kill a bill. The chairman can decide who gets to offer testimony at the hearing. It could be very one-sided.

But, for the sake of our discussion, let's assume the chairman agrees to take up the bill, orders the hearings, and they are relatively fair. After the hearings are concluded, the chairman may have to send the bill to a budgeting committee to study it for its possible cost. This may also take some time to complete, or it could also kill the bill at that point. Again, let's assume that the bill returns to the Education Committee scored for cost. It is now ready for a vote by the Committee.

Keep in mind that a vote at this point isn't necessarily a straight "up or down" vote. Members of the committee may be allowed to add amendments, offer substitute provisions, or re-write the bill in some other way. This has led, in the past, to legislators voting against the final version of bills they authored because what they were left to vote on was totally different from what they sent to a committee. But, again, let's assume the bill survives fairly intact to the Committee vote. Once the vote is taken, the Committee will report the results to the full chamber of the legislature. For our example, let's also assume the Committee vote was in favor of the bill.

At that point, it is up to the Speaker of the House to decide what to do next. He can also put off any further votes on the legislation if he chooses. Assuming that doesn't happen, a vote will be called for on Congressman Smith's bill. If it fails, it dies right there. The whole process will need to start over again if it is to be considered further. If it passes, it is one step closer to becoming law. But, it still has a long way to go yet. To continue our discussion, we'll have our bill pass the House.

Congressman Smith now will find a member of the Senate to sponsor his, or a similar bill, in the Senate. The same process will go on in the Senate that we just described. But, the Senate has another device to use to stop the bill that the House doesn't. It is called the Filibuster. If at least 41 Senators agree, a vote will be prevented in the Senate on the bill. They can effectively block any legislation with this procedure.

If the Senate version of Congressman Smith's school choice bill passes there, the next step is called Reconciliation. Leadership from both houses will appoint a temporary Conference Committee comprised of equal members of each house. Usually the party in power of each chamber will have a majority of its members on the committee. The Conference Committee's job is to compare the two bills and make sure they are basically the same. Oh, also at this point, members of the Conference Committee can modify the bill and add whatever amendments they want to it. When they have a finished product, they will vote on it in the Conference Committee. Assuming it passes, it is sent back to both houses for further consideration.

If Congressman Smith's bill makes it this far, it is now known as a Joint Resolution. Both Houses need to vote on it again. If it passes both houses, it is then sent to the President. The President has the option to sign it, veto it, or do nothing (known as a "pocket veto). If the president signs it, the bill finally becomes law. If the President vetoes it, it can still become law if both houses of the legislature vote via two-thirds majorities to override the President's veto. The Constitution gives the President 10 days to decide what to do. If he does nothing – the "pocket veto" – the bill becomes law after the 10 days without his signature. We'll have our bill be signed into law by the President. So, now, school choice is the law of the land, right?

Not so fast, given our current less-than-functional government, there is one more step that might happen at this point. Some group, in this case probably a teachers' union, will file a lawsuit in federal court claiming the law is unconstitutional. A federal judge may block implementation of the law until the court renders a decision on the law. Since there are three levels of federal courts, it could take a few years for it to be finally decided upon by the Supreme Court. If the court rules in favor of the law, it finally becomes the law of the land.

This last stage has become the "out" that cowardly legislators use to avoid being seen as supporting controversial laws. This was not the intention of the framers of the Constitution. The courts were not to be considered the final arbiters of law in this nation. It was the responsibility of the Legislature to create law, not the courts. Theirs was the responsibility to offer "opinions" about the consistency of a law to the provisions of the Constitution. But, given the proliferation of lawyers in this country, and the arrogance of those will some legal education, the courts have begun to dominate the government. Even though the courts were to have been the least powerful of the three branches of government, a growing oligarchy of judicial "rulers" has taken more and more control of this nation.

But, it is totally unnecessary. You see, our Founding Fathers were no fools. They wrote a provision into the Constitution to limit the power of the federal courts. One of the powers granted to the Congress is the power to limit the courts on which issues they may consider. It is known as the Exceptions Clause. It is found in Article III, Section 2, Paragraph 2. The paragraph concludes with these words, "In all the other Cases before mentioned, the Supreme Court shall have appellate Jurisdiction, both as to Law and Fact, with such Exceptions, and under such Regulations as the Congress shall make." This is a powerful tool at the Congress' disposal to rein in the courts. But, sadly, most legislators are too gutless to use it. The left knows this too well. That's why they have used the courts to advance their secular cultural and socialist economic agendas over the past several decades. They knew they had little chance of their issues passing legislatures, so they attempted this end run around them. The legislatures allowed them to get away with this tactic.

What I'm describing is the fact that the Congress could pass legislation declaring abortion illegal. As part of the provision of the bill, they could include language that denies the courts the right of review on the law. The courts might not like it, but they would be powerless to intervene. Innocent human life would then be protected again. It sounds simple enough, but the leftist elitists in the country would howl like werewolves if they were denied the opportunity to "rule" over the rest of us peasants! But, it would be a perfectly Constitutional thing to do.

As I mentioned, legislators often will seek support for their bills to aid in passage. This is called co-sponsorship. It can be a ploy used by politicians to convince their constituents that they are truly on board with an issue without having to do any of the "heavy lifting" to get the bill passed. But, it can also be a useful tool for us to influence the passage of legislation. Here's how it works. When we hear of a bill being proposed by a legislator, we can then contact our own representative and ask them to co-sponsor the legislation. If enough people from his district make the request, it might be enough to get him on-board even if he wouldn't have initiated the bill himself otherwise. If enough people from enough districts put pressure on their legislators, it can create a movement to get a bill passed. Many politicians like to be seen as getting on-board of what they think is popular legislation.

Of course, it would be best if our own legislators would take the lead on issues important to us; if they would initiate and fight for bills. But, if we don't have a true conservative warrior representing us, we can still, again repeating Reagan – "make them feel the heat." At almost all levels of government, there are legislators who are willing to lead the charge for us on issues. But, it is up to us to provide cover for them. A lone legislator is easily defeated by the other side. These brave men and women need our support if they are going to be effective.

This business of just going along with the flow of a bill is a common tactic used by cowardly or lazy legislators. Remember the "Barney Fife" Congressman I referred to before? He always crows about being pro-life. And yes, his voting record is generally pro-life. But, he is certainly not a pro-life leader by any means. He has been in Congress now for twenty years and has yet to initiate any pro-life legislation of any kind. He's content to hop on board to preserve his job, but it is hardly an important issue for him. Real leaders will lead on issues, not just stick their fingers in the wind and see what it is they believe!

Another way to get our issues passed is to develop a strategy to streamline the law-making process a bit. This is done by getting a member of each chamber of the legislature to sponsor similar bills at the same time. Congressman Smith starts his bill on school choice in the House. At the same time Senator "Jones" sponsors a similar bill in the Senate. Both bills are working their way through the process simultaneously. Hopefully, they will both reach the Conference Committee around the same time and still look similar. If that is the case, final passage may take far less time. To be even more efficient, if we have a President who is sympathetic, he can be part of the process as well; using his influence, (his "bully pulpit"), to persuade those on the fence to vote the right way. He will also be in a position to sign the bill quickly after it is approved by the Congress.

Of course, the easiest way to get our issues passed into law is by electing enough of the right kind of people to office. It would be great if we could trust those in our state capitals and Washington to do the right thing. But, until our movement wields that kind of political power, we must work to do all we can to influence those who are in place already. Even if we can get Congressman "Smith" to vote the right way 75% of the time it's better than what he may be doing now.

We need to have key contacts who are keeping a close eye on the legislatures of this nation. Several of the advocacy groups have their own people in Washington and the state capitals. They can inform us what is happening with both good and bad legislation. We can take our cues from them as to when the most effective time is to contact our representatives. They can inform us when a piece of legislation is being proposed. They can let us know when crucial committee votes are pending. They can identify which legislators are solidly in our camp and which ones need to feel pressure from us. Remember, the right pressure applied at the right time will have the maximum effect.

This is also important for the folks we urge to share in the contacting effort. There is nothing more frustrating for people who are marginally involved than to feel their efforts were wasted. "Yes, I called Congressman 'Smith', but he still voted the wrong way." We want to best utilize our army in such a way that it doesn't burn out from a large amount of effort with a minimal amount of results. Proper strategy and timing is, therefore, crucial to improve our success rate. We will also build enthusiasm among our ranks if they see positive results for their efforts.

101

A related issue to this is the need to **be sure of the facts before we act**. A classic example of this is an "urban legend" that has been circulating around every few years for at least four decades. It goes something like this – The Federal Communications Commission is currently planning to pass regulations to stop all religious broadcasting on radio and TV. Please contact the FCC immediately to express your objection to this proposed regulations' change. Have you ever heard this? Have you signed petitions, sent letters, and made phone calls to the FCC to stop this?

Please don't be embarrassed if you have. Thousands of well-meaning Christians have been duped by this fraud over the years. The truth is there has never been any such move by the FCC. It has all been a lie. Most probably it gets initiated by groups opposed to religious programming in an effort to make Christians look stupid and alarmist. The FCC gets flooded with communications over phony regulations and then has to waste time and resources debunking the rumor. Christians become an annoyance to the FCC. The anti-religious people win a victory because they have sent the Christians on another wild goose chase. And, Christians get embarrassed and frustrated because their well-meaning involvement was worthless.

We need to be sure of exactly what is happening before we act and urge others to act. We need to verify our sources. We need to be skeptical of anything that doesn't pass the "smell" test. Remember, deceit and fraud are two of Satan's biggest weapons. We don't need to be gullible. We need to be wise and prudent in how we proceed on issues and campaigns of influence. We are people of truth! Truth always must be one of our goals.

Since we are people of truth, cursing the darkness alone can never be one of our end goals. **We must also build the good and positive, not just dismantle the evil and the bad**. Ending legalized abortion is a noble goal, but it is not enough. After we stop the murder, we must also get to the root of the immorality that leads to unwanted

102

pregnancy. We must teach our young men and women, boys and girls the value of each human life. We must teach them the positive power of human sexuality to strengthen two-parent nuclear families and, in turn create strong local communities with a code of personal responsibility. From there, strong local communities lead to strong states and strong states lead to a strong nation.

I'll give you an example of how this can work. Back in the early 90's, when I worked with the Christian Coalition, I got a call from some activists in a southern county in our state. They asked my help and advice to stop a backdoor move by a Planned Parenthood sympathizer to create the public climate for an abortion clinic in their area. The way this was being attempted was through an individual who was seeking to get permission to get a "sex survey" distributed to the largest local school district in the county. The survey, which would have been given to kids as young as 5th grade, was very explicit and probing about kids' knowledge and experience on a wide range of sexual topics.

The goal was obvious. The pre-conceived results were set to show the large percentage of sexually active teens' need for more "family planning" education and services (read – ushering in Planned Parenthood). The next step would have been the justification of an abortion clinic to lessen the number of unwanted teen pregnancies and children in poverty. It is a typical strategy the left uses to get their foot in the door to get rich by destroying lives.

I asked my contacts to call a meeting of concerned citizens. I can remember a group of about 75 showing up. The local press was there as well. I used a local newspaper story as my starting point for the evening. The headline read something like this, "Local teens are getting pregnant and experts want to know why." I held up the story, read the headline and then chuckled to the audience, "Any of you parents want to explain this to the "experts"? My point was to show the stupidity of the façade put up by this supposed group of "experts." I also explained to them the strategy that was being used on them by the pro-aborts.

We talked for some time and planned the first part of the strategy to get the school board to reject the survey. We used parental rights and the potential disruption of the learning process as our rationale for the school board to act in our favor.

But, that was just the first part of the battle. We couldn't be seen as just "against" something. We had to move towards a positive. We had to address the issue of teen pregnancy. At that point, I contacted the director of the Pennsylvania Family Institute for his organization's assistance. One of their programs was an abstinence-based sex ed. presentation called *True Love Waits*. I was able to put him in contact with the local activists. They were able to organize another meeting to gain support to promote the program in the schools. In other words, we worked to stop the deceitful attempt by the pro-aborts to gain a foothold in the schools and then took the positive step to address a real issue from a moral point of view. It was a successful effort on everyone's part at the time.

This was one example of what can happen when we work together, form coalitions, and replace a negative with a positive. But, we also need to be realistic. **This battle will not be short or easy**. The stakes are enormous. We are talking about the future of the world here, not just our own lives and families. If God is calling us in this day and age to stand up for His truth in our culture, we must prepare for a long, and sometimes bloody, campaign. We will have setbacks. We will lose some battles. We will not be able to change some things for a long time. But, the battle is worth engaging in. It is the future we are seeking to pass on to those who come after us; just as our ancestors did what they could to pass along to us a free and prosperous society.

But, take courage! **Persistence pays off!** We will see victories if we don't quit. The political left and the "country club" moderates in this country don't have our stamina. They don't have our heavenly source of strength. Most of us are used to "swimming upstream" just by virtue of living our Christian faith in a fallen world. We need to apply that persistence and hope in this arena as well. If we make changing our society our goal; don't give up no matter what the current circumstances; and trust in God's goodness to lead us, we can see a much different world in the future.

Chapter 9: Learning How to Frame the Debate

"You're a racist, sexist, homophobic bigot!" Have you ever been called that? It's not uncommon for anyone of a conservative or religious bent to be labeled with this mantra from the "enlightened" left. Actually, what they're engaging in is attempting to win the argument without having to have a debate. It is a common tactic of the culture wars, especially of the liberal side of the fight. By personally attacking the character of those they disagree with, it negates the need for them to defend often illogical or indefensible positions that they have committed themselves whole-heartedly to believing.

It is also a way to frame the debate to make their position seem more palatable to the public and make any dissenters seem extreme. Framing the debate is a crucial tactic in winning public opinion. Very often a position, or a piece of legislation, will rise or fall depending on how it is worded. That's because words mean things. Let me give you a few examples from recent history.

East Germany was one of the most repressive communist regimes of the latter half of the 20th century. Hundreds of people died trying to escape the clutches of their communist lords by attempting to traverse the no-man's land of the Berlin Wall. Yet, despite this tyranny and oppression, East Germany's official name was the German Democratic Republic! Imagine that, a place with no freedom, democracy, or republican form of government boldly proclaimed it was some kind of utopia where anyone would want to live! That's an example of how propaganda works – make something sound appealing even if it is evil to the core. East Germany was a blatant example of using language to attempt to deceive people. A few others are far closer to home.

Way back in the early 1970s, at the beginning of the war over abortion, those who stood on the side of life were naïve about their opponents. They allowed the radical feminists, the eugenicists, and the greedy Planned Parenthood types to shape the conversation about abortion. The baby-killers coined the term "pro-choice" to make their grisly act seem harmless. In addition, they labeled those who stood up for life as "anti-abortionists" or "anti-choice." The strategy was simple. Make those who revere life appear to the public as those who are the opposition to a component of freedom. Everyone likes to have choices in their lives, don't they? It's un-American to take away people's choices. This is what these simple labels were meant to connote.

They even went further in their deception and evil in describing the aborted babies as "tissue" or "product of conception." They argued that early in gestation, babies in the womb weren't human. They were evolutionary throwbacks. They weren't viable; therefore they had no real value. That's why when the dirty little secret of "partial-birth" abortions became public, the baby-killers howled like wolves at the moon. They knew that if the public ever understood that full term babies were being partially delivered and murdered while only their heads remained inside their mothers, the public would be sickened. Those in Congress whose souls have been bought and paid for by the baby-killer lobby did everything they could to keep the truth suppressed.

In the late 1980s, Rush Limbaugh attempted to re-frame the debate to some extent with his term for radical feminist abortionists. He referred to them as "femi-nazis." His point was clear. Just as Germany's Nazi party was a fascist regime allowing no dissent, so too the radical feminists really didn't believe in choice for women. They only wanted women to make one choice – abort their babies. His term drove them mad! Its parody value lasted for years. It also made some people think about what they, themselves, believed about abortion.

Another tactic the abortionists used was to skew the statistical truth. Whenever a pro-life person found themselves in a debate with a pro-abort, the pro-murder candidate would always try to paint the pro-lifer as extreme by accusing them of demanding women have babies that were the products of rape and incest. Or they would accuse the pro-lifer of not allowing for a life-of-the-mother exception. In other words, the pro-lifers were really the extremist, uncaring people. This was a "straw man" argument. The truth is that only about 2% of all abortions have anything to do with rape, incest, or the mother's life. All other abortions are done because the woman doesn't want to have the baby for whatever reason.

I always thought I would love to be in a debate with a pro-abort and call their bluff. I would say it like this, "Okay, I will support keeping abortion legal for verifiable cases of rape, incest, and the mother losing her life if she carries the baby to full term if you will agree with me to outlaw abortion for all other reasons." I know where that would lead. The pro-abort knows Planned Parenthood could never make their 300 – 400 million dollars a year if they could no longer do 98% of their business! The pro-abort would have to back track furiously or deflect the issue by calling me a name lest they be exposed as wanting all abortions with no restrictions for any reason whatsoever.

By the way, the appeal to sympathy for rape was used by Norma McCorvey's attorneys in the now infamous "Roe vs. Wade" abortion case. (She was Jane Roe.) The only problem was that even though she was coached to say she was raped, the truth is that she wasn't. It just made her more sympathetic to the courts. So much for legal ethics!

A second blatant example of framing the debate to make the false seem true is the struggle over homosexual rights. The roots of this conflict go back to the early 1970s. It is a battle still raging today. Up until the 1973, the American Psychiatric Society listed homosexual behavior as an abnormality. Then, without any clinical or verifiable scientific reasoning behind it, it voted to remove homosexuality as sexual dysfunction. Their reasoning had far more political and social pressure behind it than any science. The vote was something around 52-48 % by their members. The truth was that there was no clear consensus then. Only propaganda and attempted social engineering has changed that, not any new scientific research or breakthroughs.

The first way the homosexual political lobby attempted to reframe the debate was during the AIDS outbreak of the 1980s. The media and those in political power then did everything they could to muddy the waters about the truth of AIDS. AIDS was a disease contracted through unsafe homosexual sex. There was some carryover into the heterosexual population via drug addicts, bi-sexual behavior, and unsafe blood donation practices at the time. But, to listen to the media, one would think AIDS was going to be the next great plague of mankind; a plague that we were powerless to stop. The truth is that AIDS could have been contained and virtually eliminated if the homosexual behavioral component was dealt with openly and honestly. But, the homosexual lobby made sure there was never a hint of personal responsibility involved in dealing with it; other than promoting condom use.

As a result of the cowardice of many in society, we have spent billions and billions of dollars to deal with a disease that is 100% preventable. Sadly, thousands of poor souls have died horrible premature deaths because they have believed the lies the homosexual lobbies churned out via the media and Hollywood.

Not only has the government spent money like there was no tomorrow for efforts to fight AIDS, regulations have been put in place to insure that there will never be any kind of accountability. During the late 90s, new federal medical privacy regulations were enacted called HIPAA. Even though it will still be denied by most, the truth is that HIPAA was pushed by the homosexual lobby so that there could be no accountability for behavior. They didn't want the public to know that most of the AIDS cases involved promiscuous homosexual behavior.

The public health debate was won by the homosexual lobby because they were successful in framing the issue to make it appear that AIDS wasn't a largely homosexual disease. Once again, the propaganda of the left won the debate over the feckless efforts of the largely uninformed majority. It was commented on by a pundit at the time that AIDS had become the only disease in history with its own civil rights.

But, the AIDS controversy was only one of the early battles in the whole culture war over homosexual rights. Another cogent example of framing the issue as far as homosexual rights is concerned is the term "homophobia." This word began to be coined in the early 2000s as a way to silence dissent about the creeping influence the homosexual lobby was making into most areas of society. The word sounds like a valid science-based, or at least psychiatrically-based, word. But, the truth is it is purely an invention of homosexual proponents to label those who disagree with them.

Let's look at what has happened with this term. The second part of the word – "phobia" sounds like a mental health diagnosis. A phobia is an irrational fear. People with phobias need counseling and/or therapy to be "normal." Hence, anyone who disagrees with the homosexual agenda must need counseling because they have an irrational fear of homosexuals. That is what the use of the word is meant to accomplish. Those who criticize homosexual behavior are "sick" and in need of counseling. As a result, most people don't want to be viewed in that unfavorable light, so they keep quiet. Those who do speak out are labeled with the term and their ideas and arguments are summarily dismissed. There is no need to listen to them since they are "homophobic"!

Let me emphasize as strongly as I can; the word "homophobia" and its derivatives are not the result of careful psychiatric or scientific study. It was a culturally-invented word, plain and simple. It is nothing more than a tool of the homosexual lobby and its activists to deflect attention from their philosophy and behavior.

As a result of lack of "push back" by those in society who know homosexual behavior is destructive spiritually, economically, socially, culturally, and legally, the battle for homosexual rights has become more and more militant. Not content to simply be given "live and let live" status, today the homosexual advocates are pushing all of traditional values as far off the mainstream stage as they can. They started first with "civil unions" and homosexual adoption laws. Now they are demanding the recognition of homosexual marriage, a homosexually-integrated military, and homosexual curriculum be mandatorily taught at all levels of school. Yes, one can only wonder how long it will be until the next kids' movie will feature a Disney princess named "Steve"! Oh, that's right, I think one of the *Shrek* movies has already given us that!

My point is that we are now fighting a defensive war against this destructive behavior because we did not challenge the issues aggressively when they were first foisted upon us. We did not counter the propaganda attempts effectively and have now allowed the deceptive language of the left to appear as "normal."

These are just two examples of our recent culture wars where we have given away ground needlessly because we were outflanked by the left in their use of language specially designed to deceived and warp the minds of the masses. I could cite similar examples in the battles against the radical "global-warming" environmental fanatics and the inflammatory language still employed by the class warfare and race-baiting leftists. They, too, have used propaganda to get and hold their parasitic positions in the greater society.

My point in all of this is to advise us to be wise in how we engage in the debate. Not only do we need to be trained to spot and avoid the propaganda terminology of the left when we debate, but we also have to learn to frame our issues in their best possible light. We stand for the truth! We need to be able to express it simply and forcefully. It needs to go forth with common sense and in a fashion that includes rather than excludes people. We don't need to go through all of the semantical gymnastics to get people to believe our views like the left does with their lies. It should be an easier and more straightforward task for us than for the left. Remember, we don't need to put any lipstick on pigs!

We need to look with fresh eyes at our beliefs and positions. I'm in no way suggesting compromise or deception. There is no need for either. What I am urging is that we couch our views in the kind of language that will be most effective in winning the masses. Most people in this country are conservative in their views. Most people in this country have a belief in God and a three-fourths majority identify themselves as Christians. Our task isn't difficult. It involves two components: clearly expressing our views and exposing and refuting the erroneous views of the left.

To do the first, we must know the language of the masses. We must know how to communicate with the maximum number of people effectively. One of the mistakes I think we often make is to try to appeal to people with jargon they don't understand. Remember, our society has been educated with left-wing propaganda in our public schools for the last 50 years. We can't expect people to always be rational, logical, or consistent in their beliefs. Most have never been taught to think. The educational models employed over the past few decades have been affect-based rather than intellectually based. In other words, we've taught students how to get in touch with their feelings but not how to think for themselves! Johnny may be stupid, but at least he feels good about himself!! Our goal is to figure out how to get through to people on both an emotional and a rational level. For all of our issues, there are both intellectual and emotional components. We need to use both aspects in our arguments. In short, we need to appeal to both their hearts and minds.

We also need to be careful how we use our "religious jargon." I'm not suggesting we don't appeal to Biblical authority. Of course the

Bible is our ultimate source of truth. However, we can speak Bible truth without using direct Scriptural quotes when needed. I remember a Christian performer some time ago parodying a church person witnessing to a non-believer. It was both funny and tragic at the same time. He began with the Christian asking the potential convert, "Brother, have you been washed in the blood?!" The response was, "Oh gross! I hope not! Why would I want to wash in blood?!" The parody went on through several more "churchisms" and the confused responses. The point was clear — when communicating with people who don't share our faith, we can't expect to get through if we only use Christian lingo.

The same is true with our issues in public discourse. We have to speak in a language where we can be heard. Even though the Bible is the inspired, inerrant, authoritative Word of God; for those who haven't believed or submitted to it, it holds very little authority. But, all the same, people may believe a great deal of its truth without realizing it. We need to find the common ground and go from there.

Another part of winning the debate is to make sure we are relevant. An acquaintance of mine told a story some years ago of when he first ran for county sheriff. He appeared before the local political party gathering to garner their endorsement of his campaign. When he got up to speak, he used his time to describe, in graphic detail, the horrors of abortion. What he said was all too true, but all he succeeded in doing was turning off most of his audience. Since he was running for county sheriff, it was unlikely that he would have to deal with abortion as part of the duties of that office. Instead, he should have touted his law enforcement experience, his commitment to honest government and his desire to have his local sheriff's office run efficiently and effectively. He never got the endorsement and didn't win the election. What he got was an education about what works and doesn't work. At last I knew, he is still very pro-life and still tells that story to advise people to be wise in what and how they present their issues.

A dove tail to this point is the fact that we need to understand that public policy and government are not good forums for evangelism. God created the church to evangelize the world, not the government. He created government to order society in such a way as to be tranquil and secure. Each has its own sphere of influence and priorities. Government makes a lousy Church and the Church is terrible at trying to usurp government authority to enforce belief. Both are necessary and both are designed to work arm in arm, but if we want to evangelize the world, we need to use the Church as our vehicle, not the government. Of course, the government should support the Church's effort in this. And, of course, the Church should support the success of good government and speak out against inefficient and corrupt government.

The second component of this battle is learning how to destroy the false arguments of the opposition. Since we are Christians, we need to be able to do this without resorting to personal attacks and corrosive destruction of the debate. Even those we consider most despicable are still made in the Image of God. He still loves them even if they are lost and deceived. We need to view our opponents as God does. Secondly, we want open honest debate. If we throw firebombs back at them, it becomes a contest of zingers, not a substantive debate. We want to use the opportunity to not only defeat our opponents, but also to educate the masses. It is a cheap lazy trick of the left to use extreme language to silence the opposition. They don't want people to really think about what they are advocating. They just want people to like or trust them more than us. They are all about image over substance. We are about truth. Truth needs no public relations firm to make it appealing if we present it in the right way.

But, the first thing we need to be prepared for when debating the left is the effort to reframe the debate from the beginning in such a fashion as to allow them to win by default. It could be the format. It could be the setting. It could be the audience. Although we may be willing to go into the lion's den, just surviving isn't the goal. It is winning hearts and minds. If we are confident that the setting is somewhat neutral, then we can proceed more forcefully. (Although, the reality is that no one is neutral and objective. Everyone is influenced by their pre-conceived ideas and world views.)

Secondly, the left is good at using all kinds of slight-of-hand in presenting their issues. They will speak generally about their positions, not allowing any tangible examples which may be refuted. Very often debates degenerate into specific criticisms of our positions all the while ignoring glaring problems within the leftist argument. We must insist that the debate be equal on the level of comparison of the issues. We cannot argue theory on the same level with practice and experience. A position may seem wonderful in theory, but in the real world, it may fall apart. An example of this is the often heard argument about all the killing that's been done in the name of Christianity over the centuries. It is true that, at times, the Church overstepped its bounds by using force to coerce belief. That has always been wrong. But, those who raise the issue are themselves hypocrites. They will usually spout some socialist dogma to show its superiority. But, the truth is more people have been slaughtered by secular regimes in history many times over the totals they cite for Christians. Communist empires slaughter people as a matter of course to consolidate power and to intimidate and subjugate their masses. And, the numbers of innocents slaughtered by Muslims in the course of their history still is far greater than the two previous groups combined. No, we must make sure we are debating apples against apples; not apples against watermelons!

The left will also often use the "straw man" technique to win. This involves erroneously describing the opponent's position and then proceeding to knock it down with one's own points. They miss-characterize our views and then destroy the caricature. For example: "All of you pro-lifers want to put women in jail who've had abortions. But, we who are pro-choice want to give women the freedom of conscience to make their own life choices." This is phony because pro-lifers don't want to put women in jail who've had abortions. We want them to have loving counseling to rebuild their shattered lives. And, most pro-aborts want women to "choose" to have abortions. That's the only real choice they want women to make. When was the last time you heard a pro-abort praise a woman for having a baby?

We must avoid falling into the "straw man" trap at the outset. To do this we must first call them on their error. Then we must correctly describe our position. That should negate their argument. But, then we are primed to fire back with a challenge to their points that are inconsistent or deceptive. Now, they will be on the defensive and we will have gained the upper hand. A good book I recommend about this type of debating and spotting other techniques used by the left to win arguments unfairly is *Discerning Truth* by Dr. Jason Lisle.

We must always remember that our mission is to bring forth truth. That truth may be about marriage. It may be about economics. It may be about American History. It may be about life. Our goal is to present it to the public in such a way that they identify with our views and reject the radical views of the left, no matter how deceptive or sugar-coated they are presented. In order to do this well, we must learn how to frame the debate to our advantage. As Dr. Jason Lisle puts it, "Remember, our opponents aren't neutral; and we shouldn't be either!"

Everyone who advocates for a specific position of public policy or societal norm has an agenda. It may be philosophical. It may be economic. It may be personal. The motivation may be secondary, but we must realize the bias that is present when we engage in the debate. To do other is to admit defeat before we even open our mouths to give our position. If we are not prepared for this, or recognize it, we will represent our views poorly, weakly, or without clarity.

We must go into public debates ready to enunciate our positions clearly and as positively as possible. We can't just be against homosexual marriage. We also have to be for healthy spiritual hetero-sexual marriages. We can't just be against raising taxes on the "rich."

We have to be for the economic freedom and fairness of free market capitalism that enables everyone to prosper at some level. We can't just be against the gross abuse of power being usurped by federal judges. We must be for honesty, common sense, and real justice in our legal system. The list goes on and on, but my point is that we can control and define the debate if we appeal to what everyone essentially wants – fairness, integrity, and common decency in society. We will show ourselves as being worthy of the stewardship of the public trust in opposition to the professional pandering politicians and radical lobby groups that are destroying this nation. Nineteenth century evangelist D. L. Moody once said, "The best way to show that a stick is crooked is not to argue about it or to spend time denouncing it, but to lay a straight stick alongside it."

We need to study our opponents, their positions, and their tactics. Once we understand their deception, their limitations, and their tired old strategies, we will find them far less than invincible. In fact, we will see them as weak. It's like the difference in watching President Obama speak with and without his teleprompter. Take his prepared words away from him and he is the Wizard of Oz after Toto pulls back the curtain! The same may also be true for many other advocates of the left's agenda. Their positions are built on houses of cards. Take away one of their carefully crafted arguments and their whole position collapses.

When we learn and practice these strategies of framing the debate, we may even start to enjoy these thorny confrontations! We will be able to explain our positions without feeling defensive, frustrated, and at a disadvantage no matter what public arena in which we may find ourselves. We will be bold, confident, and exactly where God wants us to be in winning hearts and minds. We may even find ourselves trying not to chuckle when the left goes into hysterics after they are trapped in a corner of logic from which the inevitable conclusions of their own positions have backed them! When all the left has remaining to them is name-calling, then the old adage we learned as children will come to mind. "Sticks and stones may break my bones, but names will never hurt me!"

Chapter 10: Learning How to Win the Public Debate

It was the summer of 1990. I boarded a bus early in the morning and traveled the 3 ½ hours to Washington D.C. I was on my way to an expected gathering of pro-life people called the Rally for Life '90. I was on the chartered bus with a variety of people from my home area – young and old, Protestant and Catholic, blue collar and white collar. We were all headed to our nation's capital to show our support for life. I wasn't sure what to expect. I didn't know how many people would show up or how successful the event would turn out.

My questions were answered when we got into the city. We were jammed in with traffic. By the time we got to RFK stadium, our bus parking place, the parking lot was overflowing with busses, emptying and empty, from people who had come there from several states in the Union. As we made our way to the nearest Metro station – heading for the National Mall, the crowds grew larger and larger. By the time we got off at the Federal Triangle, we were pushed along in a moving river of humanity – all heading in one direction. As I approached the Mall from behind the Washington Monument, it was already crowded with people on the hillside. I continued up over the hill and, finally reaching the crest, my eyes were shocked by what I saw.

From the top of the Washington Monument hill all the way down to the Reflecting Pool and to the base of the Lincoln Memorial was a solid sea of humanity! This was before any other memorials were constructed there, so it was virtually all open space; at least it would have been had not hundreds of thousands of people been occupying the lawn! Only the sidewalks were visible. This was the largest group of people I had ever seen in one place.

Needless to say, the rally was a huge success. We heard speeches and music for hours. Celebrities, government leaders, and pro-life dignitaries all took their turn to inform, motivate, and entertain us. All 50 states were represented. People came from all over the world. An absolute cross-section of humanity was present. I saw people of all ages, all races, all creeds, and all nationalities. There were Catholic priests and nuns, Greek Orthodox monks, Jewish Rabbis, Protestant clergy, and all other sorts of people. There were people in their 80s and 90s. There were newborns in strollers. Banners, signs, and streamers by the thousands waved in the breezes of that hot Washington summer day.

By the time it ended, I was exhausted. I slowly made my way back through the crowds to RFK to find my bus. When all the riders were accounted for, we headed back home slowly; fighting traffic for at least the first two hours. When I finally got home it was very late.

Before I went to bed, I thought I'd check the news to see what kind of story the event had gotten. Now, remember, this was long before Fox News, the Internet, and Facebook. My news options were limited. CNN was the only cable news in existence. To my dismay, the news media largely ignored the event. What small stories they did mention reported the crowd at just around 100,000. I know they were there. I saw news cameras, reporters, and photographers all over the place during the day. So, what happened to the story?

Sadly, this was my first real lesson in media bias. I found out the next day's edition of the Washington Post, the home town paper, didn't even put the event on the front page. What picture they did include was of a single family with a stroller on a large open patch of grass. They didn't even show one crowd shot. I don't know where the photographer found that much grass to include in his picture! The numbers they were reporting were laughable. 100,000? I've been at professional sporting events in stadiums where the verified numbers were around 50,000. I can tell you the crowd I saw, and was a part of, was at least ten times larger than any stadium crowd I have ever seen. It was probably over 600,000, conservatively estimating.

What I learned is that the national media will not report the truth about issues they disagree with. Abortion has always been a divisive issue in our country ever since a liberal Supreme Court "invented" new rights in the Constitution in 1973. To be for life is not politically correct. I didn't realize, until then, the lengths the media were willing to go in distorting, hiding, and lying about the truth on this issue. They truly embarrassed themselves on that day. They proved just how incompetent and ideologically driven they really are.

The Rally for Life '90 was the largest rally on the Mall since the great 1960s civil rights gathering. History alone merited reporting about it. But, the press didn't want the rest of America to see just how deep and broad the support for life really is in this country. A few weeks later, there also was a large gathering on the Mall – a gathering of radical pro-abort feminists. The press couldn't help tripping over themselves to promote and report about this rally. They reported the numbers at 250,000. The crowd shots I saw showed a much smaller gathering than the one I attended. But, that didn't matter. The story was written even before the event happened – the feminist abortionists outnumber the pro-life religious extremists!

I tell this story and its fallout to make a serious point about our winning the culture wars today. We cannot assume the truth about who we are and what we believe will ever be reported in the national press. Today, they are propagandists for the left. Rush Limbaugh calls them the left's stenographers! He is all too correct in this description.

It is true that today we have more news options than ever before, but we still have to be cautious about trusting national media to be honest and accurate with us. Fox News was a breath of fresh air when it made its appearance on cable TV. Finally, we thought, accurate news reporting that tells the whole story. We even tolerated Alan Colmes' silly ranting's opposite Sean Hannity because it seemed they were trying to be fair. But, I found out we couldn't just sit back and relax now that Fox was here.

In 2009, Tea Party activists and concerned citizens from all over the country marched on Washington in droves – probably the largest crowd ever in the nation's history. I saw the video and the still pictures. Now, I've walked those streets. I've been on the Mall several times. I know how much humanity it takes to fill those spaces. The estimates of 1 ½ to 2 million were not out of line. I was dismayed at Fox's reporting of the numbers at "tens of thousands."

I was further disgusted with Bill O'Reilly when he said he thought the numbers were around 75,000. I couldn't believe Bill could be so naïve to believe whoever it was who fed him that number. All he had to do was look at the aerial photographs and compare them with an aerial photograph of RFK Stadium in the area. Just the stands of RFK hold 55,000. If the football field were filled with people too, it would be easily over 100,000. All he had to do was compare crowd shots to the same scale aerial picture of RFK and he would have clearly seen the number – 75,000 – was at least off by a factor of ten!

I stopped watching the O'Reilly Factor after that. That saddened me because I had previously liked and promoted O'Reilly. In fact, I had a small contribution to his early success. My family was randomly chosen as a Nielsen rating family in 1998, during O'Reilly's beginnings on Fox. Because I saw him as a potential powerful voice for the truth, I gave him the highest ratings possible. I listed his show at both the 8 and 11 p.m. airings every day we were logging our viewing. But, somewhere along the way, his drive for fame and success has compromised him. His show was already starting to become more and more risqué with "puff" pieces by that time, so I was already not watching him as regularly as I did earlier. This gross distortion of the numbers finished me off as a viewer.

The challenge we face today in transforming our culture with our involvement is to not allow the media to define us. As much as possible, they will ignore us. When that fails, they will attempt to marginalize us. And, when that fails, they will paint us as dangerous extremists. We will never get a fair hearing from them. We will never be their "friends." We will never be able to trust them to be fair and accurate – so strong is their bias and bigotry where people of faith are concerned.

If we want to get our message out, we must realize that we have to do that job ourselves. We must create our own channels and communications networks. We need to find a way to speak directly to those who support, or would potentially support us. We have to be our own spokesmen. We have to create our own rebuttals to the lies and distortions that are, and will continue to be, leveled against us. There is no other solution to this problem. There is no easy fix; no quick answer.

Our movement needs to become media savvy. On the TV front, we must support and encourage the Christian news outlets like the *AFA Channel, NRB*, and *CBN Newswatch*. These and others are available to anyone with hi-speed internet connection via the *SkyAngel Network*. We also need to develop more and more of our own TV news sources. All of our people need to have reliable, timely information that is free of the liberal bias we have endured for decades.

We also need to plug more people into news sources not on conventional cable. The internet can be a great source if we use a bit of discretion in whom we trust to bring us news. A few examples that I have found include *One News Now; World Magazine Online*; and *Newsmax*. Others may follow. Many ministries have a news component to the information they disseminate. This is the case with *American Family Association* and *Wallbuilders*. If we search out these sources, we can develop a reliable network of information that we will never get from the TV networks.

If we are seeking a news magazine that is usually reliable, I recommend *World* magazine. It is very much styled like *Time* or *Newsweek* magazines; but without the blatant bias to liberalism. In fact, it has been decades since I wasted my time reading those two. We need more magazines like *World* today. I used to think *Christianity Today* was a worthy publication, but since they have gone the way of following the Neo-Evangelical movement (which is neither new nor evangelical), they have lost their credibility. Today, they are simply espousing the same re-warmed social gospel of the liberal church of the 1960s.

Another source of news can be email alerts and newsletters from the various ministries working to change the culture. We can forward these emails to all of our contacts. We can copy the newsletters and supply the copies to our churches. This is all part of being a resource person for information to those within our sphere of influence. **Remember – "Knowledge Is Power"!** The left wants as many ignorant, uninformed people in this nation as possible. They are far easier to control if their attention is only on reality television rather than what is really happening in the world. If all who think like we do are brought up to speed on what is happening, we can be far more effective in our responses.

We may even have to get into the print journalism business a bit ourselves. We may be able to find alternative sources for national news, but often our local newspapers, TV, and radio stations have the same liberal biases as the national media. Remember, they have all gone to the same journalism schools. If we want a fair shake at the local level, we may need to create local newsletters for people in our communities. A high-tech version of this would be local news websites that we administer and fill with information.

I have certainly seen the need for this in my own area. The local newspaper – the only one in our county – is always in the tank for our local US Congressman. I mentioned him previously – *Barney Fife* who went to Washington. No matter what he does, he always gets positive press about it. That is largely due to the fact that he is the "hometown boy." His district goes well beyond our county, but they want to do everything they can to keep him in office. As I mentioned previously also, he is a third-rate Congressman who never really does anything important. But, that doesn't matter to the paper. He is "one of us."

The good news in all this is that we don't have to fully reinvent the wheel. We also have a number of conservative, though not necessarily Christian, news sources out there. We can take their information with a grain of salt, but often they provide us with valuable information. We may disagree with them on some issues, but where we can agree, they can provide us with valuable information readily at our fingertips. I will give some examples of these along with a list repeating those mentioned in this chapter at the back of this book.

As we are more effective in getting the truth out, we will begin to win the public debate on the issues. Most people sincerely want the truth about things. The number of "Kool-Aid drinkers" in this country who are willingly blind is a minority. We may never reach them. But, the truth is we don't have to convince everyone. We just need to convince enough people to win elections and transform the government. When the benefits of a limited, moral, Constitutional government are experienced by the people of this nation, success will only build upon itself.

In the meantime, we need to convince everyone we know to stop watching network news, most cable news, and some local news sources. We need to steer them to the sources we already have and those sources we will develop that give the truth about the issues. We need to show skeptics and sincere seekers that what they have been seeing is far from the whole story. We also need to remind them of just how biased their news sources are.

Let me remind you of a recent example. Herman Cain was tried and convicted in the news of sexual harassment charges from unnamed, unsubstantiated sources. To this date, people still don't know what it was he was supposed to have done. But, that didn't matter. Literally hundreds of news stories were done about his guilt and unfitness for the Presidency.

Now, let's contrast that with a few liberal politicians. Former Democrat Presidential hopeful and former U.S. Senator, John Edwards, had an affair and a child with a woman while his own wife was battling cancer. The national press resisted that story for months until they were forced to cover it. The allegations were true. All has now been admitted, but they didn't want to damage one of their own.

A few years ago, it came out that the Rev. Jesse Jackson fathered a child with a staffer he was in a longtime adulterous relationship with. When the story finally broke, Jackson stepped down from his organization for a weekend of "counseling." He returned to head his civil rights organizations the next week. The press quickly moved on to other things. Jackson still is one of their "media darlings", so nothing further was reported. No more accountability was demanded of him.

Finally, most of us would like to forget the spectacle of Bill Clinton's Presidency and its multitude of scandals. The press seemed to think that perjury before a grand jury is acceptable as long as it's lying about sex. They all marveled at his ability to tell lies with a straight face! Clinton came within a whisker of being removed from office. Senior Democrat Senator Robert Byrd had his speech written calling for Clinton's ouster. He was just minutes away from delivering it on the floor of the Senate when he was "gotten to." Clinton survived infamy by just a handful of Democrat votes. What the press failed to report was the fact that Clinton operatives, working with seedy pornographer Larry Flint, threatened to expose a number of sitting Senators' own sexual misdeeds if they went ahead with the impeachment conviction.

Where was the Pulitzer Prize winning journalism on these scandals? It didn't exist because the American press had sold its soul to the liberal agenda in this country. This has only gotten worse today.

The people of this nation can no longer have any faith in the so-called "main stream" press.

I could cite many other examples, but my point is made. We need to have honest, fair, balanced, and thorough news sources. We can't wait for others to do it for us. We have to get the word out to all the people we know about where they can get the real story on issues. Most people don't want to have to work to dig for the truth. We can help them immensely if we point them in the right direction.

We can win this public debate, but only if we change the rules about who gets to report the truth. We don't need to be frustrated. We don't need to allow the liberal press to define us. We can push back until the majority of the people in this nation really hear the truth. Remember, truth is what we are all about. Let's do all we can to share the truth to set people free!

Chapter 11: The Most Effective Ways to Contact Public Officials

All elected officials need to know what their voters think about issues. Some sincerely want to know where those they represent stand on issues so they know which issues to support and which issues to oppose. Others just want to know the percentages of support and opposition on the various issues so they can craft their positions, frame the debate, and justify their votes. They may not really care about a particular issue, but if they believe it is important to a majority of their constituents, they will pay very close attention to it. It is only a minority of public officials that will vote how they want regardless of what the voters' think.

Knowing that these statements are true, it behooves us to know how to maximize our voices to influence our representatives to vote for and support issues important to us. In order to do that, we must learn how the system works and how elected officials evaluate input from those who put them in office. The ways to do this are bad, good, better, and best. Of course we want to do it the best way possible whenever possible.

Part of our consideration for contacting public officials is determined by what level of government they are on. If we have an issue with a local parking ordinance, a quick phone call to the mayor's office may solve the problem. But, calling the White House to tell the President how we feel on some national issue is probably not going to accomplish much. Of course, personal contact with our elected officials is nearly always the best course of action. It isn't always feasible or practical for us to do so, however.

During Presidential campaigns, voters love and candidates' campaigns loathe town hall meetings. The voters love them because they get to speak personally to potentially the most powerful man in the world. Campaign managers hate them because they can't control what is said during them. Their candidate could look unappealing depending how he comports himself with these "real people."

Candidates and elected officials who genuinely care about people never mind face to face discussions with constituents. This is the most effective form of communication with those who want to represent us. If we can get an appointment with our Congressman, or can attend a town council meeting, we can often be effective in promoting our position. **Speaking face to face and one on one when we are promoting an idea allows the elected official to ask questions and dialogue with us about what we are advocating.**

Some time ago, I lived in an area where a "mom and pop" phone company had existed a number of years before. They had been bought out by a large national phone company. But, they kept some of the older inefficient services of the mom and pop company in place. One of them was the fact that I had to dial the area code first in order to make a phone call to the next town – just a few miles away. It was the same area code, but was a different local prefix number. It was a pain to have to dial the extra numbers every time I needed to call anyone in this town. I complained to the phone company, but got nowhere. They were making money with the more expensive long distance calls, so they had no reason to change. (This was before internet phone service, by the way.)

Since I figured that the phone company was under the authority of the state Public Utility Commission, I contacted my local State Rep. I got an appointment in his office and we sat and talked about the problem. He understood my issues and realized that I was one of many constituents affected by this lack of service. He told me he would contact the PUC and see what they could do. I did get a response back from a PUC official later saying that they were going to look into the matter at later hearings. I moved out of the area not long after that, so I don't know if it ever got resolved, but the fact was that I was able to set a chain of events in motion to have the problem investigated.

Attending local town council meetings is also a great way to be heard. Usually, anyone can speak at them. Sometimes the discourse is a complete waste of time. Sometimes it is very important to our lives. I lived in a small town once that was facing a real problem. The bordering township had zoning authority over a tract of land overlooking the town. It was wooded, undeveloped land. We had gotten word that a company that tested explosives wanted to move in there and set up a facility. The catch was that they needed a zoning variance to do so. We knew that if they were to locate there, it would be a real negative for our community. So, what could we do? We weren't residents of the township that had to make the decision. We were just neighbors. A discussion was had at our town council meeting as to how to proceed. We decided to enlist the aid of all of the neighboring communities. A meeting was scheduled by the township to discuss the matter. As is the law, it was an open public meeting. We got the word out to people from all around the area to attend. The township meeting was moved to the local high school auditorium in anticipation of the crowd.

By the time the meeting began, the auditorium had over 500 people in it. About a dozen different people spoke in opposition to the zoning variance. The group representing the explosives testing company was certainly intimidated. The whole thing concluded after about an hour. No decision was made immediately. The township supervisors delayed their vote on the matter. After the meeting, we sent letters-to-the-editor to the local papers. Some people did interviews on local news stations. Gossip began to spread that the supervisors had been bribed. They began to deal with irate neighbors. Within a couple of weeks the decision came down – the zoning variance was denied. The threat to our community was averted! We later managed to convince the owners of the property to sell it to the state Game Commission to increase the public hunting lands in the area.

We can accomplish quite a bit at the local level if we take the time to show up for the public meetings and express our opinions. It often gives us the opportunity to educate both the public and those in local government our views on things. It will also serve to inform our neighbors that we are people who are involved and who know what's going on. This local involvement may have long-term benefits that we don't see at present.

Many times we may not be able to speak directly with elected officials, especially U.S. Reps and U. S. Senators. So, how do we get our point across to them effectively? First of all, we must understand that anyone serving in government at that level gets hundreds or thousands of communications each and every day. Between social media posts, emails, phone calls, and letters, they can be inundated with people expressing their opinions. This doesn't include the pressure groups and their *robo* calls and *robo* emails pretending to be real people.

If we want to be most effective in getting our point across, we must know the best ways to do it. Calling a Senator's Washington office if we are from another state may make us feel like we are doing our part, but it ranks low on the influence list. We will be most effective in contacting our own Senators and Representatives. We are their constituents; the people who have the power to make or break their political careers. A liberal Senator from another state may be despicable, but he has no fear of us if he knows we can't vote against him next election.

So, that is the first key. **We must know who the men and women are who represent us directly.** They are our primary targets on any issue. We need to compile a list of addresses, emails, social media, and phone numbers of all of our representatives from the local, state, and federal levels. For the state and federal levels, we should have both the listings for their local offices and their state capitol and Washington offices. When we need to communicate with them, it may be necessary to contact them at both their local and main offices.

Phone calls are a good way to express our opinions. When we do so, we should try to contact their local offices first. Since people tend to call the main offices at state capitals and Washington first, the numbers of calls there are often very large. They are also less meaningful. Usually, people will call a Washington office from anywhere in the country to express an opinion. The call will be noted, but just added to a "pro' or "con" tally for an issue. But, if we call the local offices of our representatives, the call will hold more weight. The people working there don't have to deal with nearly as many calls, so each call is given more priority. Most representatives will be in communication with their local offices to see what responses are coming in even if they are in Washington or the state capital.

When calling the local office, clearly identify yourself and where you live. Make sure you mention that you are a constituent. It is also helpful to mention if you voted for the representative in the past and whether you will consider voting for them in the future based on their voting record. Be polite and courteous. Do your homework. Know what you are talking about. If you know the specific number of the legislation you are expressing your opinion about, give it to the person on the phone. That will let them know that you are an informed voter who is watching them. Accountability can be a terrifying thing for a professional politician!

If your issue is pressing at the state capital or Washington; and a vote is happening shortly, you may not have time to contact the local office to be heard in time. If that is the case, call the state capital or Washington office. At least your voice will be added to the numbers of the calls they are getting. It is not unknown for large numbers of people to call Washington and "crash" the Capitol switchboard!

If there is an issue coming up that you have time to respond to more thoroughly, a letter to your representative is the best way to go. Again, it should be sent to the local office with a return address showing it is coming from one of their constituents. **The most powerful is a**

hand-written letter signed by you. That tells your representative that this was important enough for you to sit and take the time to correspond about it. Many, many advocacy groups send sample form letters or emails to their members that are just duplicated and passed on to the right representatives. These have a little weight, but require very little time and effort. They are treated as such by those in government.

One of the basic rules of thumb in communicating with those in government is that the more personal the contact, the more powerful and potentially effective it is.

It is also necessary to do follow-up communications with your representatives. If they ultimately vote the way you wanted them to vote, communicate a thank you phone call, email, post, or letter to them. They need the encouragement when they do what is right. They also need to know you were watching them. If they vote against your position, send them a polite disappointment communication. Remind them (again politely) that you will remember this vote when the next election comes around.

Another cardinal rule when it comes to communicating your views with your elected representatives involves relevance. You may want to express your opinion on an issue to a representative, but if it isn't one they are dealing with at the moment, they will largely ignore what you have to say. They have more important things to focus on at the moment. You will get a polite form letter back from them stating that they thank you for your opinion and they will keep your views in mind when the issue comes up. I know. I've gotten my share of those kinds of letters in the past before I knew better.

To be the most effective, communicate with them on an issue that is presently before them for consideration. To do this you must be informed about what is being considered in your state capital and in

Washington. If your issue is pressing, they will pay attention to what you have to say, whether they agree or not with you.

Sometimes representatives will hold public meetings on issues. That is your golden opportunity to have your voice heard. Plan to attend one or more of them. Always be polite. Do your homework before you go. Know what you are talking about. An opponent, whether in the crowd or the representative themselves, will know it if you aren't prepared. Also, remember you are sharing your opinion with both the representative present as well as the public. That may mean the people in the room as well as any press stories that follow. Who knows how far your opinion may travel or how many people it will influence? You want to give it your best when you have such an opportunity.

So, then, let's summarize:

1. Be polite and professional. Even our opponents will respect us more if we show that we are rational and serious.

2. Do your homework. Know exactly who it is you need to contact concerning the issue. Know enough information about the issue and possible legislation to assure the representative that you know what you are talking about.

3. The most effective way to communicate our views with those elected to represent us is through face to face meetings and conversations. These may take place in the representative's office – one on one. Or, they may take place at public meetings where many others might be witnesses to what we have to say. In either case, there is the possibility of dialogue, asking questions, and clarifying both our and the representative's positions.

4. When we seek to communicate a position to a representative we must focus on being relevant to the issues they are dealing with at present. Giving our opinions about issues they don't have directly before them will accomplish very little.

5. If possible, when communicating via phone, email, or letter; contact the representative's local office first. The communication will have far more force. Always remember to identify yourself and make it clear that you are a constituent.

6. When writing letters, a simple hand-written one signed by you has the greatest impact. You're communicating, "This is important to me!"

7. If a vote on your issue is immanent, contact the representative's state capital or Washington D.C. office. The local office may not have time to send on your communication.

8. Don't forget follow-up communications. Thank the representative if they voted for your issue. If they voted against it, politely remind them you will keep that in mind the next election.

9. Attend council meetings and town hall meetings whenever possible. It is a great opportunity to communicate your views with not only the representative, but also the people present and anyone else who sees or reads the press report.

10. Don't give up. It may take more than one attempt to be heard. Remember Jesus' parable of The Persistent Widow!

Chapter 12: Should I Run for Office?

This book would be incomplete without taking a good look at this question. I have been emphasizing the fact that involvement is for everyone all through this work. But, does that also include urging everyone to run for political office as well? **The short answer to that question is a qualified "no."** As I stated previously, holding elected office is a calling of God; just like a ministry office is in the church. No one should seek to get elected to public office unless they feel a definite calling from God to do so. As with any calling of God, holding public office requires a special person; one God is equipping to handle the task successfully.

Now, having said this, **I also want to encourage everyone to pray about whether God is calling you to run for some office**. He is raising up an army of believers to engage in the public arena. That certainly includes those who need to hold public office, not just advocate from the outside. This nation only functions properly when its government offices are filled with honest sincere people who are motivated by patriotism and informed by truth. Christians certainly fit in this category, so it is a logical conclusion that God is calling people today to run the government.

Our government needs good people at the helm from dog catcher to President. It may well be that you fit into one of the offices perfectly well. It may also be God's intention to train or grow you into a particular office because He knows you will do a great job there for your fellow man.

We Christians have far too long allowed "dirty politics" to be done by others; many of whom didn't deserve our support. It is high time we roll up our sleeves and get our hands dirty in order to fix the mess we see today in government. Being part of a government can be an effective way to accomplish that.

So, how should we proceed? **First of all, it must become a matter of serious prayer. We need to ask God if he wants us to get involved at this level. Second, we must ask Him to guide us as to which office we should seek to fill. Third, we need to ask Him to send people into our lives who can provide counsel and guidance to us.** We need the wisdom and accountability of others if we want to clearly understand God's will for us in this. Only after we have worked seriously through these three steps are we ready to proceed. My assumption is that if we work through these steps, we will have the answer to the question of this chapter. But, that is only the first step.

Getting elected to office doesn't just happen. It takes much planning and work beyond the hours and hours of prayer necessary. It also takes a certain level of common sense. I've had many a conversation over the years with people trying to convince me that they, or their candidate, were the ones the Lord wanted in a particular office. In some cases, they made sense. In many others, they did not. For example, it is highly unlikely that the Lord is going to call someone with no political experience and is not known by large numbers of people to become President of the United States. It is also highly unlikely that the Lord would call an unknown to run for the U.S. Senate in their first attempt at political office.

What is far more likely is that the Lord may be calling someone with no political experience or political following to run for local school board or town council. That way, the newcomer could learn both how elections and campaigns work as well as learn how to govern a small group of people on local issues. It may well be preparation for greater things. Or, it may be just that the Lord knows this person's talents are needed locally to fix everyday problems in a community.

It is also far more likely that the Lord might speak to a state representative to run for U.S. Representative, since they already have some experience in elections and the legislative process. It is far more likely that the Lord would call a state senator to run for Governor. Or, that the Lord would prompt a U.S. Senator or state Governor to run for President.

My point is that the Lord will prepare us for the offices we need to fill if we trust Him and do it in His timetable, not ours. We already have far too many incompetent people running our states and national governments. Remember former House Speaker, Nancy Pelosi, the third in line for the Presidency, telling reporters it was necessary to pass the health care bill in order to know what's in it?! Not only was that incredibly deceptive; it was also incredibly stupid!!

I could go on and on with examples of sheer idiocy in our elected officials. It helps to explain the mess we are in. But, many of you already have seen and heard the examples I could give. The bottom line is that God's plan isn't just to get more Christians into elected office. His plan is to get more competent honest Christians involved who will work to fix the current mess. This requires preparation and experience. This takes time.

It also takes an army of people willing to get involved in public office. Who knows where a run for town council may eventually lead? Carol Mosely-Braun was a Chicago city clerk who became a U. S. Senator from Illinois (Not a very good one, but she is an example of someone gaining a great level of political achievement). Mark Schweiker was a county commissioner in Pennsylvania. In the mid-1990s he was tapped to be Lieutenant Governor of the state. After 9-11, Tom Ridge was asked to move on to head the new Department of Homeland Security. Mark Schweiker then assumed the office of Governor of Pennsylvania.

Many other examples could be given of people who started humbly and then moved on to far greater things. There is no way to know what God has in mind. But, everyone had to start somewhere. **Maybe the Lord is calling you to begin a path of service that will result in big changes to this country?**

By starting with prayer, you put yourself in a good position to hear God's voice. If we are open to His leading, instead of asking His stamp of approval for our own will, He will guide us. By evaluating and praying about the needs of your community politically, you may find opportunities you hadn't previously considered. And, by enlisting the counsel of friends that you trust, you may learn more about your strengths and weaknesses before they are put under the microscope of public scrutiny. Since your friends really care about you, they will hopefully give you the frank honesty you need in your consideration. Remember, you want support that is honest not just flattering. Politics is filled with "yes men" that all have their own agendas. You are not served by sycophants. **A real friend will tell you the truth even when you don't want to hear it.**

This group of friends may well be the beginnings of your prayer team to hold you up when you become convinced that you should run for office. They may evolve into a trusted inner circle of advisors for you. Only a fool thinks he knows everything about being a leader. The best leaders want to hear diverse opinions; even opinions opposing their own views.

When Ronald Reagan came into office, one of his agendas was to improve education. He selected William Bennett to be his Secretary of Education. Bennett quickly drew the harsh criticism of the entrenched elite educational establishment in this country by challenging the status quo. I remember the story Bennett tells about his first Cabinet meeting with the President after receiving some very public ridicule from the press concerning his views. He thought he was going to be "taken to the woodshed" by Reagan for sure. Reagan began the meeting by referencing the press criticism of Bennett. He looked at Bill and said something like, "You're really stirring things up, aren't you?" Bennett thought He was in for it now, but instead Reagan turned to the others on the Cabinet and said, "So what's the matter with the rest of you?"!

One of Reagan's strengths was his ability to surround himself with quality advisors and then trust them to perform well. We need to have the same kind of people around us. They will look out for our best interests as well as look to be our partners in change. We may not always agree with them. And, we can never just rely on the opinions of others to guide our lives. We have to put the pieces together between our interests, our abilities, our leading from the Lord, our counsel from friends, and what opportunities may present themselves in order to know what we should do. By the time we get to that point, we may well have clear direction as to whether we should run for office and which office we should seek.

Assuming we have worked through these steps and have decided to run for office, **we must be ready to commit 100% to our efforts. Anything less will result in failure**. I learned that some years ago when I was working to help a guy run for Congress. He had the right background, the right education, and the right likeable personality to do the job effectively. He was right on the issues. He seemed like a "good horse to back." But, as we got into the campaign, it became clear that he had no understanding of the work and commitment involved to succeed at that level. He wanted to remain in his regular job. He didn't want to spend the time fund-raising that was necessary. He wasn't willing to put himself "out there" to become known by large numbers of people. He resisted the advice I gave him as well as that of his paid consultants. I remember one day some weeks before the Primary Election, when things were starting to get intense, he asked me which Congressional Committee he should serve on. At that point I knew it was over. He was looking for the prestige and notoriety of being a Congressman, but had little will to do the hard work to get elected. He finished third in a field of four Primary candidates. The winner lost badly to the incumbent in the fall General Election.

Part of wanting to serve is also "calculating the cost" in advance. To run successfully for any office will require time, treasure, and effort. No one is "anointed" to political office. Everyone must do their best to get there. Many will do whatever it takes to get elected. We must do things in an honorable way if we want to be the Lord's representative. Our ethics will constrain us from engaging in some political strategies that others might employ. That makes the need for us to redouble our honest efforts to win elections. God has given us rules to follow that others in politics choose not to obey. That doesn't mean we are at a disadvantage. It just means we have to work harder, know the issues better, connect with people more personably, and show ourselves to be worthy of people's votes.

I have seen many an incumbent lose re-election because they became corrupt or lazy in their position. The power of elected office will always attract people with various motives. Anyone in office who believes they *deserve* to remain there is asking for a huge surprise come election day. Some of the silly and stupid things politicians have done are almost beyond belief. But, power corrupts and they became out of touch with reality.

Part of counting the cost for a potential political career involves the cost to family. You cannot even think about getting into politics full time without the complete support of your family. They will be asked to make sacrifices. Their lives will be put on display. Remember beer-guzzling Billy Carter or drug-dealing Roger Clinton?

A family is part of the candidate in today's election lexicons. It appears now that no one and nothing is off limits. Will your family be ready for that? Will they be strong enough to stick together when it hits the fan? If the answer is "yes", then go for it. Adversity can often make families and leaders stronger. If you know you have a spouse, children, and/or siblings you can count on no matter what, you are truly blessed.

We might make any number of justifiable criticisms of the Kennedy family, but when it came to supporting one another, they were a tight knit bunch. Even when William Kennedy Smith went on trial for rape in Florida, "Uncle Teddy", Senator Edward Kennedy flew down from Washington to testify for him. Ok, ok, the thought of Ted Kennedy being a character witness for anyone is laughable, but he did what he could to support his tarnished nephew.

My point is we need to have strong family backing to do this job. The higher up the political ladder we climb, the more important this truth is. If you can't rely on and trust your family, who else will you be able to rely on when things get difficult?

An extension of this is your church family. **You need a strong network of Christians supporting your efforts. You need people praying for you constantly**. You need people telling their friends and neighbors the truth when the press stops being your friend and casts aspersions on your character. You need people to keep you grounded and humble. You need people to lift you up and encourage you after spending quite a bit of your time in the lions' den.

Another thing to consider if you are going to run for office is the fact that any sins of your past will most probably come out. That is especially true, the higher the office you ascribe to having. Your opponents will employ "opposition researchers" to overturn every rock. I remember back in 1994 when Rick Santorum was running for U.S. Senate against Harris Wofford. Santorum's campaign found the Chicago police mug shot of a much younger Wofford after he had been arrested for protesting at the 1968 Democratic National Convention. It was one of the campaign's more light-hearted moments.

This truth has to become part of your equation if you are considering running. To think you can keep things secret, especially things that are of public record, is foolish. Assume all of your past will come out in one way or another. This is also true for your spouse and other close family members. It wasn't widely reported, but prior to the 2008 Presidential Election a story was broken about the fact that Michelle Obama had been given a $350,000 plus job at a major Chicago hospital. That was after Barack was elected to the U.S. Senate. When he chose to run for the Presidency, she resigned the job and the Chicago hospital immediately eliminated the job. Even though the sympathetic national press chose to ignore the questionable employment, it was still uncovered.

None of us is perfect. Many good leaders have had flaws in their past. Having made mistakes doesn't disqualify you for office. It just means you have to own up to your mistakes. Tell the simple truth. Ask for people's understanding. And, then move on to the future. People will forgive past problems. They tend not to forgive those who try to lie about and cover them up. Just look at Bill Clinton. He will never have a legacy as a great, or even good President because of his cover-up attempts for his multiple scandals.

My point is, **if there are issues connected to your past, be honest about them**. Be the one to reveal them rather than some reporter seeking a Pulitzer. Make sure your wife and family know about anything that might harm you or the family. Plan a strategy together about how to deal with them before they come up. The press will hound anyone they can to get a sensational headline regardless of the truth. Remember, most of the national press aren't religious. Few will be constrained by common decency if they think there is a scoop in it for them. Just look at what happened to Herman Cain. The press exploited his political inexperience and lousy campaign guidance to the point of hounding him out of the Presidential race. Once he was gone, his accusers crawled back under their rocks. Their lawyers went back to chasing their ambulances. And, nothing further has been heard from our supposed "guardians of freedom."

Another thing that is absolutely necessary for successful campaigns is the assembling of a good campaign team. You must have a variety of experienced, hard-working, dedicated people behind your efforts. No one can successfully micro-manage a campaign. You need to have people you can trust to get the job done. If you are seeking a state or federal level office, you will need polling people, financial people, campaign strategists, grassroots organizers, press savvy spokesmen, legal advice, an army of election day volunteers and supervisors, and a bunch of other people you can turn to for aid. Now, this doesn't mean you need to hire all of these people to full-time jobs. But, it does mean you need to have these resource people at your disposal. You will need someone to do opposition research on your opponent. You will have to have people to help you frame issues and create powerful speeches and debating points. You will need schedulers and people to man the phones. You will need people to staff the campaign headquarters and deal with the general public. You will need people connected to donors of means.

A very prudent piece of advice I can also give is to **never underestimate your opponent.** In political terms, this is the "be ye wise as serpents" part of Jesus' exhortation in Matthew 10:16. This is especially true if you are dealing with an opponent without scruples. Your opponent may engage in strategies to win that you might find despicable, pathetic, and downright dishonest. But, unless someone has the will to bring him to task, he will get away with it if he isn't stopped. Dick Morris wrote a book about Bill Clinton where he revealed why Clinton continued to engage in so much corrupt and sleazy behavior. His answer as to why he did - "because he could." In other words, no one had the moral authority or will to make Clinton accountable for his actions, so they went unchecked and probably are continuing to this day.

You need to anticipate what dirty, underhanded tactics your opponent may use against you and prepare for them. Your response will determine how successful smear campaigns are. Newt Gingrich attacked the attempted Democrat smear of his past by challenging the competence of the reporter who tried to make it a main issue of a debate.

When Democrat-hack-posing-as-objective-reporter - George Stephanopolous - set up the Republican field with his "straw man" issue of banning contraception, Mitt Romney, and the others to a lesser extent, failed miserable to challenge George's credibility as a member of the press. Much of the hub bub about contraception would have never materialized if Romney and others nipped it in the bud and saw it for what it was the moment it was raised.

Remember, **we cannot expect to get fair treatment in today's media climate**. We must be able to do the leg work they are too lazy, uninterested, or too ideologically corrupt to pursue. If we don't stand for ourselves, no one else is going to do it for us. Yes, it involves extra work for us, but in the end, it will make us stronger candidates and more thorough in our influence. It will also make would-be opponents think twice before engaging us in future smear campaigns.

No one can predict the outcome of any election. You have no way of knowing whether you will win or lose. God doesn't always tell us his purposes for our lives, so a leading of the Lord to run for an office doesn't necessarily guarantee a win. It may well be that the Lord is using the experience in your life to prepare you for something different. It may well be that your first, or second, or even third attempt will be unsuccessful. But, someday you may reach the goal of being elected. Or, God will use the lessons you have learned to motive and support others.

We must look at every election and every political opportunity as a team effort. We are all in this together. God may assemble His team in a way we could not predict. For each of us, the mission is very simple – do our best to be faithful to whatever role we have in this effort. If we can look back at the end of the day and be satisfied that we have done our best, worked our hardest, behaved in an honorable manner, and treated those around us with respect and truth, then we will have no regrets regardless of the outcome of any one election. God will honor our efforts if this is our goal and approach to political involvement.

Finally, **we must keep the prayers coming no matter at what stage of the campaign we are**. The effort must be bathed in prayer. As Paul says, "We wrestle not against flesh and blood . . ." If we are to win the political battle, we must win the spiritual battle first. Satan has had things his way in politics and governments for far too long. He is not going to give up ground easily. We are foolish if we ignore the spiritual component of this battle. If we want to free the people of this nation from the growing governmental tyranny, we must unleash the powers of heaven to fight by our side first. **Remember – Pray, Pray, Pray! That's more powerful than any super PAC's money!**

May the Lord guide your consideration of running for office. May He bring the right people into your life for support, encouragement, constructive criticism, and guidance. And, may He bless your efforts and hard work as you seek to serve Him in this calling. If you have all these things working for you, there is no limit to the transformation that can take place in this country!

Chapter 13: What's the Long Term Goal?

So, what does victory look like? What will it be like to live in an America where our foundations are restored and God is welcomed in society rather than shunned? In other words, when can we say we have accomplished all of our goals and objectives?

The short answer to this last question is, "Never!" **Present victory is never a guarantee of future successes. Freedom always involves vigilance.** Truth can never be taken for granted or it can be easily lost. No one electoral victory or passed piece of legislation can guarantee future benefits.

When Bill Clinton and the Democrats won control of two of the three branches of government after the 1992 election, people thought that they would control government for decades to come. But, given broken promises and multiple scandals, by 1994, the American people had enough and voted in a Republican Congress to check his power and expose his corruption. Newt Gingrich and many conservative legislators reined in an out-of-control government for several years.

After the Democrats took back Congress in 2006 and the White House in 2008, the press was ready to proclaim the death of conservatism and the rise of a new socialist America. But, once again, broken promises, arrogant scandal, and shoving an unpopular healthcare bill down America's throat led to the tsunami response of the 2010 elections as the Democrats lost control of the U.S. House and just about lost the Senate. The up-coming 2012 election will decide if the backlash will continue by the American people or if it will fall short. It may well again come down to how many dead people vote in Florida, Chicago, and Philadelphia!

But, getting back to my first two questions – what will a transformed America look like if we succeed on all fronts? First of all, it will look like the Mall in Washington D.C. after the Park Service has cleared away the tons of trash left behind by a leftist rally – fresh and clean again! In other words, **the first change to our nation will be cleaning up the huge mess that liberals have created across this nation.** Every area and strata of our society has been polluted by secular socialist thinking and programs. Getting rid of them is the first sign of new hope for our land.

Economically, it means cutting down the size of government to the place where we not only don't spend more than we take in, we actually begin paying down the massive debt we have accumulated. It means cutting taxes. It means revolutionizing the way we take in revenue. No longer can we tax success. No longer can we hide taxes and fees in other legislation. No longer can we pay able-bodied people for doing nothing. No longer can we have worthless programs and departments designed only to employ political hack bureaucrats and buy votes. No longer can we have legislation that is intentionally so complicated that it is designed to make trial lawyers rich for generations.

The surest, quickest way to economic stability and growth is to repeal income and business taxes and replace them with a simple flat, or national sales tax. (I agree with Dr. Walter Williams' concern in that we must first repeal the income tax amendment or we are in danger of the government having double taxing vehicles.) By taxing consumption rather than production, it brings everyone into the tax system fairly. Rich people will still pay far more in taxes because they buy more stuff than poor people. Businesses will prosper because the emphasis will be on production rather than avoiding tax liability and regulation compliance. **More jobs will be created by this move than all of the combined government jobs' programs in the entire history of our country!** And, best of all, it completely takes the government out of the loop as to which businesses succeed or fail. No more special tax breaks for Senator Smith's pet projects. No more punitive taxes on businesses that are politically incorrect. No more government bailouts for companies that are run inefficiently. No more government loans to phony green energy companies. No more IRS intimidation of businesses that are on someone's "enemies' list."

Now, that is not to say that government has no role in monitoring business. **Good government will always be needed to prevent fraud.** Government will always have a role to protect consumers by demanding that businesses be honest and above board with consumers as to their products and services. But, beyond that, the consuming public will decide which companies succeed or fail. If people decide they want to pay four times as much for a CFL light bulb with toxic Mercury in it than for a simple incandescent bulb; that will be our right. But, the government will not be dictating to people how they must light their homes!

If people decide they don't want to pay $4.00 a gallon for gasoline and would rather have the Keystone Pipeline bring Canadian oil to us rather than sell it to China; that will also be our right. If people decide to access the centuries of coal, oil, and natural gas still within our borders to keep energy costs low rather than wait until the sun gets hot enough to make solar power feasible or pond scum refineries become more than a novel idea of environmental extremists; that will also be our right.

Yes, putting *We The People* back in charge of consumption and taxation rather than corrupt entrenched politicians will transform this nation for the better. Think of how much money would be available for all citizens if the government wasn't this all-consuming fiscal vampire, sucking the life out of us!

It requires a complete change in thinking about government spending. Instead of the government deciding how much it wants to spend and taxing us accordingly; we will consume as much as we want and provide the government with the tax money we want it to have. We will decide how big the government can get, not the politicians, lobbyists, and lawyers. **They will have to live within our budget, not have us become slaves to theirs!**

Now, I can just hear the liberals howling! What about the poor, the elderly, the sick? Who will care for them? They will use the same old phony charges against us that we want children to starve and grandma to eat cat food. But, the truth is that, in this system first of all, there will be far less poor and neglected than we currently have. Since the socialist mindset most recently dug in its heels in 2006, the numbers of those in poverty in this country have increased at an alarming rate. It has been totally unnecessary.

Second of all, if we have to pay far fewer government employees to run and administer government social programs, there will be much more money available for private charities to help the truly poor and needy. All government social programs are grossly inefficient compared to charitable organizations. The reason is obvious. **Charities exist because people have compassion for their fellow man.** Government programs exist because government unionized workers want easy jobs with full benefits, fat pensions, and perpetually dependent constituents. The Church and other private charities can do the job far better and cheaper than any government program can.

These are just a few examples of the new economy that will flourish when we succeed. If we think about it, I'm sure many other examples of change will come to mind. No more property taxes to pay for schools. Far too many seniors have been forced to sell their homes and move into government subsidized housing because of educationally-dependent, ever-escalating property taxes.

No more exorbitant energy taxes on gasoline. Right now we are paying between fifty cents to a dollar for combined state and federal gasoline taxes. With the amount of money those taxes raise, every street in America should be paved in gold! I could go on and on, but you get my point. If we can get government to spend money like the average responsible consumer does, all of the nation's economic woes will be fixed.

Another sweeping change will be in education. For the past seventy years, our educational system in this nation has become more and more secular, leftist, and mediocre. Teachers, administrators, and professors have become more and more well-paid and less and less accountable for the job they do. Education has become a socialist's dream! Performance of students and graduates??? . . . not so much! Public school teachers are given tenure after just a few years of teaching. Imagine, being 23 – 24 years old and having a guaranteed job until retirement! After that, they get a fat pension and health insurance until the end of life. And, the teachers' unions have virtually guaranteed that no lousy teacher will ever be fired.

New York City schools right now have about 5,000 teachers who have been judged unfit to be in a classroom. They report to a "rubber room" every school day and sit around doing who knows what all day. They are given full pay and benefits and will receive pensions upon retirement. The city can't get rid of them because of the union contract provisions. The union wants them there because they draw full union dues from them. The Democrat politicians want them there because they know that a good portion of those union dues end up in their re-election campaigns. The only losers in the whole deal are taxpayers and children. It is a deviously destructive, but brilliant money-laundering operation for the left.

Tenured college professors can say whatever they want to say, treat students any way they want to treat them, and too many have very lazy work ethics. The secular university is a dungeon of political correctness for all who attend there. Forget freedom of thought and conscience. Unless students tow the socialist, multi-cultural, tolerance line, they are ostracized and some are even denied degrees. This is especially true today in the science disciplines. Anyone with a creationist view of the world is considered ignorant and bigoted.

Despite the fact that these students do all the assigned work, some are being denied degrees or recommendations simply because of the arrogance, intolerance, and anti-religious bigotry of professors and university officials. And yes, the few conservative, creationist professors that still exist are being "weeded out" through various legal and illegal methods. Just watch Ben Stein's movie - *Expelled* - if you don't believe that is true.

Education certainly is a huge area we need to transform. **All truth is God's Truth. God is the Author of all that is true and real. We Christians have generally always led the way in education.** We need to reclaim that birthright. We need schools and universities where all is discussed and explored. We need to look at real evidences for our origins. Let the creationist and evolutionist both give their best evidence. The problem is that now the evolutionist gestapo on college campuses refuse to debate honestly because their own positions are so weak, students will see right through them.

I'm certainly not suggesting that liberal, socialist professors be removed from teaching. Theirs is a point of view that should be discussed. I'm suggesting balance. I also firmly believe that once people use their brains to consider the differences between our positions and that of the socialists, they will see the plain simple truth of ours. Besides, as Rush says, we need to always keep a few liberal professors on campuses so that people are always reminded of what liberalism really is. It's like keeping Nancy Pelosi in Congress. We need to keep her there as the poster girl for the left. People always need to see how idiotic and brainless political socialism becomes when it is put into practice in the real world!

We need to develop an educational system in this nation which isn't hostile to our faith. We need discussions about God, Jesus, and the teachings of the Bible in schools and colleges. Christianity built this nation. It built the western world. The Bible is the most produced book of all time. Our faith surely has a place in any educational program. I'm not suggesting that we use public education as a way to pressure children to convert. Evangelism is the purview of the Church, not the state. But, discussions of ethics and morality and societal behavior cannot happen fully without including Christianity. To exclude it is to grant the religions of humanism and atheism carte blanche in shaping the next generation's minds. We've seen the plethora of social problems explode because we've been shut out for decades. **It is time for our voices to be heard again in the classroom just like they were in this land for 350 years!**

We also have to have real school choice in this nation. Parents, not government, are ultimately responsible for the education of their children. If they want to home-school, that's their right. If they want their kids to go to religious schools, that's their right. If they want them to go to public schools, that's their right as well. It is not fair to force all taxpayers to support only one option. Give all parents tax credits (assuming we don't have the flat tax), and let them spend their money wherever they wish for their children's educations. Tax credits are better than vouchers because vouchers still involve government bureaucrats in the approvals and distribution. Credits are far more efficient and keep parents more in control.

Yes, teachers' unions and the politicians whose leashes they control will howl at this idea. But, that's too bad. Maybe they're scared of the market-based accountability they would face if it comes to pass. Schools would have to compete for students and wouldn't keep ineffective teachers on staff. Only the best teachers would teach. Those that did would be paid well for their professionalism. No one would mind paying a good teacher what he or she is worth. It's the substandard ones that are mucking up the system. But, as I previously stated, it is a money and power issue with the unions. That's why they pour millions of dollars into political activity each year to defeat school-choice initiatives.

Another area of needed great change is in Law. Our judicial system today is certainly broken. It is filled with too many that are greedy, incompetent, corrupt, and arrogant. It reminds me of the old joke: "Why do so many federal judges hate God? Because they don't like the competition!" Sadly that's too true. We have unaccountable judges making up laws as they go along today irrespective of what the people, the legislatures, or the executive branch wants; and what the Constitution allows. Instead of judges interpreting the laws of the legislature, they often create their own with no previous precedence.

I have had my personal experiences with the deficiencies of the legal system. My family has owned a farm since 1860. In 1972, a lawyer bought the adjacent farm for a mere pittance of what it was worth. He bought it from a man whose two children he had represented in court as a public defender some months before. In 1974, exploiting an unknown mistake in county tax maps, he claimed a large portion of our farm as his. The first we knew of his "acquisition" was two years later when his surveyors showed up and proceeded to place wooden stakes in our front yard!

My grandmother, a widow, owned the farm at that time. She engaged both a surveyor and a lawyer to fight for our rights. What ensued was a twenty year legal battle, tens of thousands of dollars spent, and three trips through PA's appellate court system until it was finally resolved in our favor. My grandmother never lived to see the final resolution.

My father, her only child, died at a young age. In fact, when this case began, there were five of us living at the farm - my grandmother, my also widowed mother, my sister, my brother, and I (the three of us all minors). When the farm passed to me, it became my ongoing fight.

The bottom line in the case was that the neighboring lawyer couldn't prove his ownership of the property. Although he did try through a mysterious new deed description, not based on a land survey, after he filed his deed in 1974. When asked by my attorney in court who created the deed description without a survey, he fumbled around for a while and then claimed it was my grandmother's surveyor who had created it! Conveniently for him, neither my grandmother nor her surveyor was in any condition to be available to refute his claim since they were both in very ill health by that time. But, since criminality and fraud couldn't be proven, no further action could be taken. Someday, the Lord will judge him for seeking to defraud a widow and her family.

More recently, a federal judge by the name of John E. Jones, III issued a ruling against the Dover, PA School District position on teaching Intelligent Design along with evolution. He ruled that I.D. isn't real science and can't be considered next to evolution. This ruling was very sad and disappointing, though not unexpected.

John E. Jones, III is from my home county. He was a "country club" establishment Republican. He came from a wealthy family. He opened a law practice in the county. In the 1980s he ran for the PA State Legislature in a heavily Republican district. He was so not liked that a conservative Democrat took the seat for the first time in decades. Later, in the early 1990s, he ran for U. S. Congress against the previously mentioned "Barney Fife" Congressman. He also lost. His greatest margin of loss came from his home county. Later, he heavily financially supported Tom Ridge's bid for Governor. Sometime after Ridge became Governor, Jones was appointed to head PA's Liquor Control Board. After 9/11 happened and Ridge was tapped to be Director of Homeland Security, Jones was appointed to a federal judge's position by President Bush. He currently still holds the position.

My point in all this is to show that here is a man with no judicial experience at any level, who was twice rejected by his own neighbors for political office, who managed to acquire a position of power in this nation. His ruling belies his inexperience. In 2008 the World Humanist Congress gave him an award. In his acceptance speech, he blamed the Dover District for not understanding Civics and the First Amendment to

155

the Constitution! His PR people sent the story back to our local newspaper; I assume because he thought we'd be interested in it. To me, he still is a glaring example of the need to fix our judiciary. **Why we would accept anyone with no experience in a position of such authority is a mystery to me!**

I'm sure many of you have horror stories of your own. We need to have judges that are just, moral, competent, and wise. We need to have judges that know our history and what our Founding Fathers really gave us in the Constitution and Bill of Rights. What we have now is destroying our culture. The role of a judge is far too important to leave it in the hands of a professional politician. We need good people to go through the law schools and prepare for a career of public service, not just get into a position to be invited to join the country clubs! **We also need a mechanism for normal citizens to hold lawyers and judges more accountable for their actions.** Anyone seeking justice is looking at a quagmire of legal obstacles. That needs to change.

But, of course with 70% of Congress being lawyers, what can we expect? **It's high time we returned to a citizen legislature.** People shouldn't be spending their whole lives preparing for political careers. People should serve in Congress from all walks of life; make their contributions; and then go back home. Guys like Richard Lugar and Arlen Specter are certainly poster boys for term limits! Thank goodness the Tea Party helped to get rid of both of them!

Another area of our society that will look different when we win is the family. The two parent family has been under societal assault for decades now. Of course that is true; socialists need weak families to justify their existence with "help from the government." The more single parent families there are; the more teenage pregnancies there are; the more unemployed high school drop outs there are, the more social programs are needed. The more social programs there are, the bigger the government needs to be. The bigger the government gets, the more tax money it needs to collect. The more tax money taken from families means two parents working or family income declining. The more financial stresses put on the family, the higher the divorce rate. Hence, the vicious cycle comes around upon itself again, thus perpetuating the problem forever.

It is time to break the cycle! **Government must become "family-friendly," not "family-hostile" as it now is.** The cultural environment needs to change to promote families and family values. These values include: fidelity in marriage, respect for parents, modesty in dress, a solid work ethic taught and practiced, faith, freedom, and participation in government, among others. Our societal goal needs to be, "what can we do to lift the quality of life up?"; not, "what can we get away with doing?"

You see, parents shouldn't have to set up blocking controls for TV and the internet. Those outlets should all come "G" rated. Let those who want other content have to jump through the hoops to see that stuff. We currently have it backwards. It's no wonder our culture is also devolving as well.

Let's have a rating system for TV commercials that match the programs being aired. I remember a couple of years ago watching a family movie – *Evan Almighty* – on ABC's *Family Channel*. It was a cute fictional account of a modern-day Noah. But, about a half an hour into the movie, a very risqué lingerie commercial came on the screen. It should have been rated TV-MA. What in the world that had any place being shown during a family movie, I'll never know. It was an assault on my family. I turned the movie off at that point. I filed a complaint with the FCC that went nowhere. This needs to be changed.

I've stopped watching the Super Bowl for the same reason. (This from someone who started watching them with Super Bowl II in 1968!) The commercials used to be highly entertaining and humorous. Now, they've become trashy. NFL teams used to have cheerleaders; now they have women dressed like strippers and streetwalkers! I'm truly sorry they have chosen to make what used to be good family entertainment into something seedy and cheap. Come on, does anyone really think that ratings would go down for the Super Bowl if the garbage commercials were gone and the cheerleaders dressed more like athletes than hookers?

We also see the same exploitation at the supermarket and discount department store checkouts. There we are, stuck in line, and we are forced to view what amounts to little better than soft-core porn in front of us. Oh, of course it is masquerading as fashion or health or entertainment magazines. But, the truth is that these magazines, with women exposing much of their bodies are a deadly poison. For women, it conveys the message that this is how they must look to have any worth or value. No wonder our little girls and teenage girls are dressing like they are selling their bodies. These magazines are telling them this is what they must do.

For boys and men, the magazines also present an equally deadly message. "This is what you must want to have", they say. "You need a woman who walks around exposing herself in order to be happy." Forget modesty! These scream, "A sleazy woman is where it's at!" Sadly, this exposure to younger boys is very much akin to marijuana. Marijuana is considered a "gateway" drug; one that leads people into harder drug addiction. These magazines are also gateway vehicles, designed to lure boys into hardcore pornography. It is no wonder we have so many absent fathers today in our families. Far too many men are off chasing fraudulent fantasies; phony fantasies incubated right there in the grocery stores.

The only reason these magazines are placed in the checkouts is money. It is assumed by the marketers that if they are right in front of us, we will be more likely to buy them than if we have to search for them in a magazine rack somewhere. Those seeking to make a profit at our families' expense don't care what harm they are doing. Many people are earning a comfortable living and even getting rich at the expense of our children and families.

These are just a couple of examples of how society needs to change to support rather than destroy the family. **This is part of our battle as well – restoring common sense social standards to our culture.** Anytime we complain about the sexual exploitation of our children, both Hollywood and the ACLU cry, "censorship!" It is high time we make them accountable for what they are doing to our families. Maybe we need lawyers to do a societal good for a change and sue them for child abuse!

One of my other pet peeves in this area is the fact that we have no rights when it comes to our cable TV choices. We have to pay for the bundles of programs they give us regardless of content. It is time to demand that TV providers give us "a-la-carte" options in which channels we buy. Of course, many channels couldn't pay their own costs if they weren't bundled together. Not enough people would watch them. But, why should we have to subsidize programming which is distasteful and insulting to our faith and families? Let the market truly dictate content. People could pay only for the channels they want to watch. Yes, Hollywood and the cable companies might not make as much money, but too bad. Give us programming we want and we will gladly pay for it! I've already previously mentioned the *Sky Angel* option that my family now has, so I won't repeat the info here.

I can't overlook the news media in this chapter on what our success looks like. **Imagine multiple news sources that are honest, conservative, and moral in their programming and reporting.** That's what can happen. No more liberal agendas. No more sleazy "puff pieces." No more distorting facts to help particular politicians. Again, I'm not saying we should censor the left. I'm suggesting we truly let the market decide and we will throw our economic weight behind worthy sources. No more government-sponsored left-wing media. The liberals could try to succeed in this environment, but I bet they go the way of *Air*

America and Al Gore's network! If the people truly had a say in what news is delivered to us, we would vote for simple truth every time.

Again, I repeat, it's not we Christians who are afraid of the truth. It is the socialist left who must use propaganda to control the flow of information. If just once, a media outlet was brave and honest enough to report the truth about what happens to a baby being aborted, this nation would turn overwhelmingly pro-life overnight! But, too much money and ideology from Hell keeps the truth silenced on this issue and others.

Imagine how powerful it would be in our Republic if the media were absolutely committed to the truth above ideology and personal power and wealth. The Press would truly be the "guardians of freedom." In fact, unless we have a journalistic revolution in this nation, freedom can't survive for much longer. I won't waste space here with the multitude of examples of media fraud I could cite. You know many of them. The doctoring of the Zimmerman 9-1-1 tape by NBC is just the latest example. Those who intentionally engage in such behavior should see jail time. They are defrauding all of us by their blind ideological biases.

Another sign of victory for us will be a significant decline in crime. The European socialist approach to reducing crime rates is to de-criminalize more and more behaviors. Obviously, that's not what I'm suggesting here. If we want crime rates to go down, we need stronger families, schools and churches. But, we also need a new philosophy of punishment for crime. It needs to be so severe that people will think twice before committing crime in the first place. I'm not suggesting the death penalty for everything, or engaging in medieval forms of torture. **But justice needs to be fair, but hard on real criminals.**

A couple of years ago, two county-level judges from Northeastern PA were convicted of abusing their power and taking bribes in the worst way. They issued harsh sentences to juveniles for even minor and first time offenses. Dozens and dozens of kids were sentenced to years at a time in a private juvenile detention center. The judges received "kick-backs" in the millions of dollars from the owners of center in exchange for sending them so many kids. The center got tons of public money for keeping their facility full of "offenders." This went on for many years before they were found out.

The judges were sentenced to a number of years in jail each for their crimes (28 and 17.5 years respectively). However, the misery they caused to so many young lives and families is far worse than what they received. What they should have received were life sentences with the requirement that they wear the prison orange jump suits and be seen regularly picking up trash alongside of the highway. Maybe then, they would finally learn what "public service" really means! They also should have been stripped of all their worldly possessions and had that money put in a fund to compensate the victims of their abuse of power. That would have been real honest justice. It would also have sent a warning message to any other public official that to betray the public's trust makes one worse than a murderer in the eyes of our society. But, given their political and possible organized crime connections in Northeastern PA, they received just a bit more than a slap on the wrist.

We see the same things happen over and over again to those in political power. When politicians, especially liberal politicians, are caught doing something illegal, they seldom receive the kind of punishment an ordinary citizen receives. **What is needed is legislation that requires anyone convicted of a crime related to the public office they hold shall be sentenced to twice the normal punishment for the crime.** Those who hold public trust should be held to higher standards; not get away with abusing the system and cheating all the citizenry they represent. After all, "public trust" should mean something in this nation. It only emboldens petty criminals if they see the famous and powerful getting away with crime.

We used to live in a society where people didn't even have to lock their doors at night. Now, we have become so backwards in our thinking that honest people need to be locked up at night and criminals wander the streets freely. When a judge is stupid enough to entertain a lawsuit from a burglar suing the owner of the house he broke in to after the said burglar slipped and broke his leg, the system is crying out for serious reform! This essential reform is part of what we need to accomplish**. It is part of restoring to our society what the Constitution refers to as "domestic tranquility."**

These are just a few of the areas I could touch on in this chapter. **We also need massive regulatory reform at all levels of government.** We need to eliminate all agencies with unelected bureaucrats having power to mandate our lives. That's where we get stupidity like the EPA threatening to fine farmers for making too much dust! Government agencies are lousy nannies we don't need. Rational, intelligent folk can figure things out on their own. The vast majority of businesses don't do stupid things. They want to be around for a long time, so they will put practices in place to help their businesses succeed now and for years to come.

The environmental extremists always want to vilify industries like logging. This is but another example of political correctness run amuck. Very few timber companies "rape" the land. They want to have trees to cut in the future, so they either "select cut," or they replant tracts they have harvested. In fact, there are more trees growing in America today than there were when the Pilgrims arrived here! Industry-led timber management strategies have created far healthier forests than would exist without human care.

No, our Founding Fathers never envisioned multiple agencies of bureaucrats telling us how to live in every aspect of our lives. They certainly didn't allow for a bank of "Czars" answerable to no one. It is only through the gutlessness of the Congress that such entities have arisen. These politicians have realized that they can avoid accountability for unpopular regulations if they can say they had nothing to do with them. That must change. We need all members of Congress to be open and honest enough to take responsibility for the laws they wish to enact. If a Congressman can't explain well enough why we need his proposed law, then maybe the law isn't worth having.

I know a number of the things I've proposed in this chapter may seem extreme to those who haven't really thought about these issues. But, the fact is these are but a few of the many changes we need to make to improve the quality of life for all in our society. That needs to be our main goal – **preserve individual freedom and liberty while at the same time promoting the best quality of life for as many people as possible in our nation.**

Yes, the evil, the corrupt, the power-hungry, the arrogant, and the lazy will never like or agree with our goals. But, that doesn't matter. Far too many of them have had far too much power for far too long. **It is time to take our nation back.** It is time to return truth, honesty, and equal opportunity back to our society.

Finally, we need a restoration of faith in this nation. We need to work diligently for a society that allows real religious freedom – the kind our Founding Fathers gave us; the kind that was espoused from Revolutionary War pulpits. Far too long now, "God" has been a dirty word in public society. We need to restore His rightful place in this land. "In God We Trust" is still on our money. It must be on our lips and in our hearts as well. That doesn't mean discrimination against those who don't believe. But, it means those who do believe will no longer be discriminated against simply because we aren't politically correct humanists.

Chapter 14: Step by Step Cultural Transformation

Ok, so how do we get there from here? We have a good idea where we want this country to go in the future. We understand the problems and possible solutions. How do we make it happen? First of all, an old proverb is relevant at this point. "How do you eat an elephant? One spoonful at a time!" That's right. We cannot expect to make the sweeping changes needed overnight. It will be a slow gradual process of improvements until things look quite different than they now are.

What I'm saying is that we must be in this battle for the long run. We cannot wave some magic political wand and expect to fix everything instantly. **Change will come slowly and gradually, but it will come if we keep on working.** Our Founding Fathers gave us a system that lent itself to this kind of slow transformation. This is a very good thing. If radical changes were constantly possible, our society would appear to be a ship being tossed violently about by strong waves. The political and societal pendulum would swing wildly to the left and then back wildly to the right. We do want to move it to the right, but we want it to move there with a steady progression that will keep it there for many years to come.

We need the time to do more than just change laws. **We need the time to change minds and hearts.** We need the time to enact long-term fixes to the educational system and the judicial system. We need to strengthen our families, churches, and communities.

This must be a comprehensive approach if it is to succeed. People from all walks of life must be involved, not just professional politicians and academic theorists. Only when we can change the nation's world-view from a secular socialist one, will we be able to replace it with our national roots of faith, freedom, self-reliance, morality, and personal excellence. When these values again hold sway in all of our institutions, then we can feel like our job has been accomplished.

This cannot happen quickly. **We must re-educate our own people first.** Far too many of us have been brainwashed by this secular socialistic thinking. We must have our minds transformed by truth. We must understand our history. We must be fully engaged citizens who know what is going on and are actively participating in our society.

Another reality we must be willing to accept is the fact that it may not happen in our lifetimes. It may well be that our generation will plant the seeds that germinate in the minds and hearts of the next generation. It may well be that today's children will be tomorrow's world changers. They may be the ones to finally turn things around.

The one advantage we have over today's lousy educational system is the fact that they are turning out substandard little socialists. Our children today, if properly trained by us, will be able to out-think, out-work, out-achieve, and out-succeed most of the products of today's public school system. We can take solace in the fact that we may well be called to train tomorrow's leaders today.

But, that also will take hard work and time on our part. We don't have to re-invent the wheel, but we need to change the flat tires on the car if we want it to go anywhere. **Our homes, churches, and Christian schools need to be "cradles of freedom" for the next generation.** If we don't start with our own spheres of influence first, we have no hope of real, lasting change.

We need to re-evaluate our beliefs, our theology, our political science, and our sociological perspective. If any of those areas fail solid Biblical scrutiny, we must adjust them accordingly. We cannot expect God's blessings for our efforts if we fail to do things His way. He has given us His Truth about how human society should operate. We ignore it at our peril. We follow it to our success.

Once we have families, churches, and Christian schools that conform to the word of God, then we are ready to move into the greater society. **Remember, Christian truths set people free.** Christian truths benefit all in society, believer and unbeliever alike. Only those bent on evil and denying God will fight against what we have to offer.

What person in their right mind doesn't want smaller government, safer streets, better education, less tax burden, stronger families, and greater opportunity to prosper? Only the parasites of our society hate what we are striving to give. Only those who feel they have the right to take from others and then control them for their own ends will oppose us.

Yes, there will always be those who are so blinded by their ambition, greed, and false beliefs that they will never consider our solutions. But, they continue to be in a minority in this nation. Look at the statistics. Despite decades of Darwinian indoctrination by the schools at all levels, we still see a majority of people believe God created the universe. Despite Hollywood's and the media's best efforts to cloud the truth about abortion, we still see a majority of Americans who believe it is wrong. There are many more examples I could give, but you get my point. **The truth will eventually come out.**

Hitler's "1,000 Year Reich" lasted only a few decades. The "communist utopia" of the Soviet Union didn't even make it a century. Saddam Hussein's revived Babylonian Empire of Iraq lasted a very short period of time. Again, I could give many more examples of societies based on secular lies that fell far short of the ambitions of the demagogues who created them. **The truth is our current flirtation with secular socialism is failing rapidly.** Either America will return to its roots and survive and flourish, or we will fade away, consumed by failed ambitions of our present political demagogues.

I'm placing my hope on the truth! I'm placing my hope on the God-given wisdom of our Founding Fathers. It's not that America can't

166

fail. She certainly can and will if nothing is done to change the course we are on. But, I still believe that there are enough of God's people here who are willing to fight for the principles that have made this nation the greatest of all in world history.

Daniel Webster put it into perspective for us, "Hold on, my friends, to the Constitution and to the Republic for which it stands. Miracles do not cluster and what has happened once in 6,000 years, may not happen again. Hold on to the Constitution, for if the American Constitution should fail, there will be anarchy throughout the world." (http://quotes.liberty-tree.ca/quote_blog/Daniel.Webster.Quote.5EF8)

Keeping this in mind, we must also understand that there will be setbacks along the way. **We cannot realistically expect to win every battle we engage in fighting.** Even the victors in war lose their share of battles. George Washington lost more battles than he won in the Revolutionary War. But, he continued on through years of frustration and privation until things finally turned in the colonists' favor. He understood that, for there to be any future for this nation, defeat and surrender were not options. We must take the same stance today. We cannot give up, no matter what the setbacks.

As the European Theater of World War II seemed to be winding down, Germany pushed back with one final offensive – the Battle of the Bulge. What had seemed like assured victory for the Allies came into question. The Germans took the Belgian city of Bastogne. Their offensive was aimed at getting to the port of Antwerp. If they could secure the port, they would have new life in the war. The Americans sent the 101st Airborne Division in to protect the city. They became surrounded. They were completely besieged by the Germans, but refused to surrender.

The conclusion to this story may have had a dark ending except for one thing. The Americans had a field commander who refused to accept defeat for his forces. General George Patton pushed his 3rd Army to get to Bastogne before the 101st was overrun. The famous story connected to this event was the fact that the weather was against the 3rd Army. They couldn't advance fast enough due to bad winter weather and with no air support possible. It was nearing Christmas.

In a now legendary move, Patton called for a chaplain, who he ordered to write a prayer for clear weather. The chaplain complied. The prayer was prayed. And, the next day the weather unexpectedly cleared! The 3rd Army made it to Bastogne in time. The 101st Airborne was saved. The Nazis were driven back and the end of Hitler's insane ambitions was soon to be seen.

My point in reminding us of this amazing and true patriotic tale of American History is that we cannot give up, no matter how things look. **What may look like a defeat may well be the prelude to victory.** If the commanders of the 101st Airborne had surrendered, none of the rest of the story would have happened. If Patton hadn't refused to accept the "inevitable", the rest of the story wouldn't have happened. If there wasn't faith for God's intervention, none of this would have taken place. (By the way, I feel certain that Patton in no way restricted his chaplain from ever praying "in Jesus' Name" as we see happening in today's military!!)

If we continue to see ourselves as God's servants in this effort to restore this nation, we cannot fail. If we act according to His example, we cannot lose. If we remain faithful to His calling, the outcome will be His to grant, not ours to fret over.

A final encouragement comes to us from an unlikely source. Thomas Paine was no friend of Biblical Christianity. However, he was used by God to inspire a generation of colonists to fight for their freedoms. The following quote comes from his second famous pamphlet – the American Crisis:

"THESE are the times that try men's souls. The summer soldier and the sunshine patriot will, in this crisis, shrink from the service of their country; but he that stands it now, deserves the love and thanks of man and woman. Tyranny, like hell, is not easily conquered; yet we have this consolation with us, that the harder the conflict, the more glorious the triumph. What we obtain too cheap, we esteem too lightly: it is dearness only that gives every thing its value. Heaven knows how to put a proper price upon its goods; and it would be strange indeed if so celestial an article as FREEDOM should not be highly rated."
(http://libertyonline.hypermall.com/Paine/Crisis/Crisis-TOC.html)

These words are true enough for our generation today. We dare not quit! We dare not surrender! We dare not compromise!

Chapter 15: Galatians 6:9

This book could not be closed out without Scriptural encouragement. I think Paul says it best in Galatians 6:9:

"Let us not lose heart in doing good, for in due time we will reap if we do not grow weary." (NASB)

Paul's original context is talking about doing good works in the church, but it certainly applies to our circumstance today as well. We must engage believing that God is behind this effort. He is fighting with us for the truth. He is fighting with us for freedom. He is fighting with us to re-establish the principles He gave to our Founding Fathers to create this blessed nation in the first place.

If we are honorable, truthful, respectful, moral and persistent in our approach, we cannot lose in the end. Remember, God loves justice. He loves truth. He rejoices when His people stand for His Truth. He blesses nations when they honor Him and live according to His principles.

Yes, we are fighting for our futures. Yes, we are fighting for the futures of our children and grand-children. Yes, we are fighting to improve the quality of life for every human on the planet. But, ultimately we are fighting to validate and proclaim God's greatness on the earth.

Paul's advice here is very important. We must not lose heart in our efforts. **We are seeking to do good; God's good.** One of Satan's tactics in stopping us is discouragement. He wants us to give up; to believe we can't change things. He wants us to doubt the cause; to ignore our responsibilities to society. He wants us to compromise our faith; to hyper-spiritualize our faith; and to so overly focus on Christ's return that we are worthless as witnesses in today's world. If we give in to any one of these lies, he will have won and we will be ineffective.

No, we cannot lose heart in doing good! **God promises us victory if we don't quit.** He doesn't tell us how long that may take. He doesn't tell us how difficult the struggle may be. He doesn't tell us how costly the price for freedom's restoration will be. But, He promises to be there with us in the struggle. He promises to give us the strength we need to carry on. And, He promises us ultimate victory in this battle if we don't quit.

Please don't think I'm suggesting that we can bring about the Kingdom of God on earth by our efforts. Only the Lord's return will put a permanent end to evil on this planet. However, we can push back and reclaim ground we have willingly or unwittingly given up to the enemy. We can see God's blessings poured out over this land again if we are faithful.

I've lived through times like this once before. When I was in college in the late 1970s, America was in a huge mess. The economy was terrible. Inflation was out of control. Unemployment was devastating. Gas lines were everywhere and one could only buy gas on the odd or even day of the week that corresponded with the last number of one's license plate. Poverty was expanding despite over a decade of billions in social spending. Abortion had been made legal. Divorce laws had become so lenient that the family was breaking down. Hollywood cast off all sense of decency and morality. Pornography exploded. The earth's climate was thought to be cooling and a new ice age was predicted. The Soviet Union was gaining more and more strength and controlling more and more of Europe and western Asia. Here in America we had a hugely corrupt Congress, dominated by liberal Democrats. We had an incompetent President in Jimmy Carter.

On top of that, we were all suffering with the humiliation of the Iranian hostage crisis. (Yes folks; Iran was a problem even back then.) It was during that time that ABC started a new late night TV show called *Nightline*. I remember huddling around a small black and white TV on dorm watching the latest news about the crisis. We all thought it would lead to World War III. We were scared to death about going to war with the Soviets.

Our President was depressed at his ineffectiveness. He hid in the Oval Office from America. We all thought this was the end for America. The future seemed bleak on all fronts.

The "end times" preachers proliferated. Many books and amateurish Christian movies were produced which declared the end was in sight. Surely the Lord would return long before the end of century. Some people in churches started selling everything and moving out of society to wait for His return. Apocalyptic cults began to grow.

But, God was faithful to His people. Many Christians began to pray; and act. Not too long before the 1980 elections, a small group of Christian activists began to work. They were known as the Moral Majority. Most people laughed them off as inept. But, they worked quietly, behind the scenes, to get people involved. By the time the election rolled around, enough Christian Evangelicals had become active politically to push the former Democrat Governor of California to a landslide victory for the White House.

Ronald Reagan, now a conservative Republican, came into office with three basic pledges – lower taxes, reduce the size of government, and defeat Communism wherever it existed in the world. He set to work restoring American values of faith, freedom, and opportunity for millions. He rebuilt the military; leading to the collapse of the formerly invincible Soviet Union a decade later. He rebuilt the economy from one of malaise under Carter to one of increased wealth for all segments of the population. He challenged Congress at every opportunity and his philosophy led directly to the 1994 conservative revolution in Congress. He instilled in America and Americans a renewed sense of pride and patriotism that had all but been lost.

My point in all of this is to point out that we can do the same thing today. Yes, it's true that we don't have anyone with Ronald Reagan's personal magnetism available to lead us today, but that is unnecessary. *We The People* **can make this happen.** We don't need a political star to shine on us. In fact, it is far better that our movement is organic and diverse rather than pinning all of our hopes on one or a few "heroes" to save us. America needs to be a place where anyone can lead effectively with the proper commitments to our heritage, our faith, and a stubborn desire to see freedom flourish.

Let me add a few more Scriptures to leave with the reader to ponder. (All are NASB)

Psalm 11:3 – **"If the foundations are destroyed, What can the righteous do?"**

This declaration is certainly where we find ourselves today. The battles we are fighting and will face are directly connected to the fact that America's foundations have been systematically destroyed over the past several decades. If we do not return and rebuild them, there will be no hope for humanity.

Proverbs 29:2 – **"When the righteous increase, the people rejoice, But when a wicked man rules, people groan."**

This statement is also very true. There has never ever been a secular utopia in all of human history. The most beneficial society that could ever exist in this world is one in which Biblical principles are applied to life. We've seen that in our nation's past. It must be our goal for the future. Having leaders at all levels of government who are "righteous" will insure the most efficient, effective, freedom-producing government we could ever hope to experience.

Proverbs 25:26 – *"Like* a trampled spring and a polluted well
Is a righteous man who gives way before the wicked."

The church today fits this description very well. Our witness has become polluted because we have allowed those who hate God to hold sway over far too many of our institutions. We must stop "giving way" to those who call evil good and good evil!

Proverbs 14:34 – **"Righteousness exalts a nation,
But sin is a disgrace to *any* people.**

God promises to exalt this nation if we do things His way. We have been far too content to be disgraced by the actions and philosophies of many in our society.

Psalm 33:12 – **"Blessed is the nation whose God is the Lord,
The people whom He has chosen for His own inheritance."**

Although this first applied to Israel, any nation that will honor the Lord will be blessed by Him. If we continue to reject God, how long do we think it will be before His judgment comes on us? If we return to His truth, how long do you think it will be before He hears from heaven and heals our land?

Isaiah 58:12 - **"Those from among you will rebuild the ancient ruins;
You will raise up the age-old foundations;
And you will be called the repairer of the breach,
The restorer of the streets in which to dwell."**

This final passage describes for us our role in what must be done. We need to repair our foundations. We need to build up new institutions. We need to transform this nation, not to the past, but to a new future, based on our faith, our Constitution, our history, and a clear vision of an America with freedom restored to its rightful place in our lives.

So, let us get to work turning this nation around because, **yes we can! By God's Grace, yes we can!!**

Addendum – 10 Things You Can Do Between Now and the 2012 Election

1. Get everyone in your church registered to vote. In most states you still have time. Unregistered voters cannot legally vote (At least, they're not supposed to vote!).

2. Make sure your church will be receiving non-partisan voters' guides before the election. Everyone in your church needs to know where all the candidates stand on the issues before they vote.

3. Set up a volunteer group of people to provide transportation to the polls for folks who don't drive or who have other difficulties getting out to vote. Announce the group's existence at your church for a few weeks in advance of the election. Provide a sign-up sheet for people to use your service.

4. Make sure any family and friends that are away at college or serving in the military have the opportunity to get absentee ballots and vote in a timely fashion so their votes count in this election. Contact your local election bureau for information about absentee ballots.

5. Put up yard signs for your chosen candidates. Put bumper stickers on all of your vehicles. Contact the campaigns or local party offices to find out how and where to get these materials.

6. Put together a calling list of family, friends, and neighbors. A day or so before the election give them all a call and remind them to vote. Also, share with them the candidates you plan to vote for and why.

7. Create your own info sheets on the candidates to hand out or place at your local polling place. Anyone can distribute literature outside a polling place provided you follow your local rules for doing so. Check your state's regulations. In my state it requires

one to remain at least 10 feet from the door of the polling place.

8. Call the local campaign headquarters and volunteer to help in the remaining days. Almost every campaign can use the help in the final push coming up to an election.

9. On Election Day, take your video camera, digital camera, or smart phone with you to the polling place. Document any voting irregularities you witness. (You may not be able to take any pictures or video inside the polling place, however.) Remember, it was "citizen journalists" that captured the uniformed Black Panthers waving night sticks outside the polling place in Philadelphia four years ago. Who knows what fraud you might be able to help curtail? I guarantee you, there will be vote fraud again this election unless we all work hard to expose it!

10. PRAY! PRAY! PRAY! PRAY! And, don't forget to VOTE!!!

Quotations

"Without justice, what are kingdoms but great gangs of bandits?" - **St. Augustine** – *The City of God* 4.4.

". . .Christian princes and magistrates ought to be ashamed of their indolence, if they do not make it (religion) the object of their most serious care. We have already shown that this duty is particularly enjoined upon them by God; for it is reasonable that they should employ their utmost efforts in assertion and defending the honour of him, whose viceregents they are, and by whose favour they govern." - **John Calvin**

"Wherever God appointed a king he never appointed him absolute, and a sole independent angel, but joined always with him judges, who were no less to judge according to the law of God than the king. And in a moral obligation of judging righteously, the conscience of the monarch and the conscience of the inferior judges are equally under immediate subjection to the King of kings; for there is here a coordination of consciences, and no subordination, for it is not in the power of the inferior judge to judge, quoad specificationem, as the king commands him, because the judgment is neither the king's, nor any mortal man's, but the Lord's." - *Samuel Rutherford*, from *Lex Rex (Law Is King, or The Law and the Prince), 1644*.

" . . . when Caesar claims divine honours, Christians must answer 'No.' For then Caesar (whether he takes the form of a dictator or a democracy) is going beyond the authority delegated to him by God, and trespassing on territory which is not his." - **F. F. Bruce**

"The state is to be an agent of justice, to restrain evil by punishing the wrongdoer, and to protect the good in society. When it does the reverse, it has no proper authority. It is then a usurped authority and as such it becomes lawless and is tyranny." - **Francis Schaeffer**

" . . . Christians, who recognize that the state's authority and ministry come from God, will do more than tolerate it as if it were a necessary evil. Conscientious Christian citizens will submit to its authority, honour its representatives, pay its taxes, and pray for its welfare. They will also encourage the state to fulfill its God-appointed role and, in so far as they have opportunity, actively participate in its work." - **John R. W. Stott**

"Back to the Bible or back to the jungle." - **Luis Palau**

"Those who will not be ruled by God will be ruled by tyrants." – **William Penn**

"Civil tyranny is usually small at the beginning, like 'the drop of a bucket,' till at length, like a mighty torrent, or raging waves of the sea, it bears down all before it, and deluges whole countries and empires . . ." – **Rev. Jonathan Mayhew (Congregational Minister, Boston – 1749)**

"It cannot be emphasized too strongly or too often that this great nation was founded, not by religionists, but by Christians; not on religions, but on the Gospel of Jesus Christ." - **Patrick Henry**

"It is when people forget God, that tyrants forge their chains." - **Patrick Henry**

"It is in the man of piety and inward principle, that we may expect to find the uncorrupted patriot, the useful citizen, and the invincible soldier. – God grant that in America true religion and civil liberty may be inseparable and that the unjust attempts to destroy the one, may in the issue tend to the support and establishment of both." - **Jonathan Witherspoon**

"Do not ever let anyone claim to be a true American patriot if they ever attempt to separate religion from politics." - **George Washington**

"We have staked the whole future of American civilization, not upon the power of government, far from it. We have staked the future of all of our political institutions upon the capacity of mankind for self-government; upon the capacity of each and all of us to govern

179

ourselves, to control ourselves, to sustain ourselves according to the Ten Commandments of God." - **James Madison:**

"We have no government armed with power capable of contending with human passions unbridled by morality and religion. Avarice, ambition, revenge, or gallantry, would break the strongest cords of our Constitution as a whale goes through a net. Our Constitution was made only for a moral and religious people. It is wholly inadequate to the government of any other." - **John Adams**

"Religion is the basis and Foundation of Government." - **James Madison**

"Providence has given to our people the choice of their rulers, and it is the duty, as well as the privilege and interest of our Christian nation to select and prefer Christians for their rulers." - **John Jay**

"God who gave us life gave us liberty. And can the liberties of a nation be thought secure when we have removed their only firm basis, a conviction in the minds of the people that these liberties are of the Gift of God? That they are not to be violated but with His wrath? Indeed I tremble for my country when I reflect that God is just; that His justice cannot sleep forever." - **Thomas Jefferson**

"In matters of religion I have considered that its free exercise is placed by the Constitution independent of the powers of general government." – **Thomas Jefferson (from his 2nd Inaugural Address 1805)**

"The highest glory of the American Revolution was this: it connected, in one indissoluble bond the principles of civil government with the principles of Christianity." - **John Quincy Adams**

"I have read through the entire Bible many times. I now make it a practice to go through it once a year. It is the book of all others for lawyers as well as ministers; and I pity the person that cannot find in it a rich supply of thought, and of rules for his or her conduct. It fits a person for life – it prepares them for death." - **Daniel Webster**

"If there is anything in my thoughts or style to commend, the credit is due to my parents for instilling me an early love of the Scriptures. If we abide by the principles taught in the Bible, our country will go on prospering and to prosper; but if we and our posterity neglect its instructions and authority, no man can tell how sudden a catastrophe may overwhelm us and bury all our glory in profound obscurity." - **Daniel Webster**

"Miracles do not cluster, and what has happened once in 6,000 years, may not happen again. Hold on to the Constitution, for if the American Constitution should fail, there will be anarchy throughout the world." – **Daniel Webster**

"The Bible is the Rock on which this Republic rests." - **Andrew Jackson**

"I believe the Bible is the best gift God has given to man." - **Abraham Lincoln**

"To the influence of the Bible we are indebted for the progress made in civilization, and to this we must look as our guide in the future." - **U.S. Grant**

"Hold fast to the Bible as the sheet-anchor of your liberties; write its precepts in your hearts, and practice them in your lives." - **U. S. Grant**

"Thorough knowledge of the Bible is worth more than a college education." - **Theodore Roosevelt**

"Thomas Jefferson believed that no king, no tyrant, no dictator can govern for them as well as they can govern for themselves." – **Franklin D. Roosevelt**

"The fundamental basis of this nation's laws was given to Moses on the Mount. The fundamental basis of our Bill of Rights comes from the teachings we get from Exodus and St. Matthew, from Isaiah and St. Paul. I don't think we emphasize that enough these days. If we don't have a proper fundamental moral background, we will finally end up with a totalitarian government which does not believe in rights for anybody except the State." - **Harry S. Truman**

"The greatest obstacle to peace is a modern tyranny led by a small group who have abandoned their faith in God. These tyrants have forsaken ethical and moral beliefs." **– Harry S. Truman**

"America was founded by people who believed that God was their rock of safety. I recognize we must be cautious in claiming that God is on our side, but I think It's all right to keep asking if we're on His side." - **Ronald Reagan**

"America needs God more than God needs America. If we ever forget that we are One Nation Under God, then we will be a Nation gone under." **– Ronald Reagan**

"A government big enough to give you everything you want is big enough to take away everything you've got**." – Ronald Reagan**

Thanksgiving Proclamation – George Washington

[New York, 3 October 1789]

By the President of the United States of America, a Proclamation.

Whereas it is the duty of all Nations to acknowledge the providence of Almighty God, to obey his will, to be grateful for his benefits, and humbly to implore his protection and favor-- and whereas both Houses of Congress have by their joint Committee requested me to recommend to the People of the United States a day of public thanksgiving and prayer to be observed by acknowledging with grateful hearts the many signal favors of Almighty God especially by affording them an opportunity peaceably to establish a form of government for their safety and happiness.

Now therefore I do recommend and assign Thursday the 26th day of November next to be devoted by the People of these States to the service of that great and glorious Being, who is the beneficent Author of all the good that was, that is, or that will be-- That we may then all unite in rendering unto him our sincere and humble thanks--for his kind care and protection of the People of this Country previous to their becoming a Nation--for the signal and manifold mercies, and the favorable interpositions of his Providence which we experienced in the course and conclusion of the late war--for the great degree of tranquility, union, and plenty, which we have since enjoyed--for the peaceable and rational manner, in which we have been enabled to establish constitutions of government for our safety and happiness, and particularly the national One now lately instituted--for the civil and religious liberty with which we are blessed; and the means we have of acquiring and diffusing useful knowledge; and in general for all the great and various favors which he hath been pleased to confer upon us.

And also that we may then unite in most humbly offering our prayers and supplications to the great Lord and Ruler of Nations and beseech him to pardon our national and other transgressions-- to enable us all, whether in public or private stations, to perform our several and relative duties properly and punctually--to render our national government a blessing to all the people, by constantly being a Government of wise, just, and constitutional laws, discreetly and faithfully executed and obeyed--to protect and guide all Sovereigns and Nations (especially such as have shewn kindness unto us) and to bless them with good government, peace, and concord--To promote the knowledge and practice of true religion and virtue, and the encrease of science among them and us--and generally to grant unto all Mankind such a degree of temporal prosperity as he alone knows to be best.

Given under my hand at the City of New York the third day of October in the year of our Lord 1789.

Go: Washington

(http://lcweb2.loc.gov/ammem/GW/gw004.html)

Thomas Jefferson's Letter to the Danbury Baptists
The Final Letter, as Sent

To messers. Nehemiah Dodge, Ephraim Robbins, & Stephen S. Nelson, a committee of the Danbury Baptist association in the state of Connecticut.

Gentlemen
The affectionate sentiments of esteem and approbation which you are so good as to express towards me, on behalf of the Danbury Baptist association, give me the highest satisfaction. my duties dictate a faithful and zealous pursuit of the interests of my constituents, & in proportion as they are persuaded of my fidelity to those duties, the discharge of them becomes more and more pleasing.

Believing with you that religion is a matter which lies solely between Man & his God, that he owes account to none other for his faith or his worship, that the legitimate powers of government reach actions only, & not opinions, I contemplate with sovereign reverence that act of the whole American people which declared that their legislature should "make no law respecting an establishment of religion, or prohibiting the free exercise thereof," **thus building a wall of separation between Church & State.** *Adhering to this expression of the supreme will of the nation in behalf of the rights of conscience, I shall see with sincere satisfaction the progress of those sentiments which tend to restore to man all his natural rights, convinced he has no natural right in opposition to his social duties.*

I reciprocate your kind prayers for the protection & blessing of the common father and creator of man, and tender you for yourselves

& your religious association, assurances of my high respect & esteem.

Th Jefferson
Jan. 1. 1802.
(http://www.loc.gov/loc/lcib/9806/danpre.html) (Emphasis mine)

References and Resources

Amos, Gary T. *Defending the Declaration. How the Bible and Christianity Influenced the Writing of the Declaration of Independence*. Brentwood, TN: Wolgemuth & Hyatt, Publishers, Inc. 1989.

Boa, Kenneth and Kruidenier, William. *Romans. Holman New Testament Commentary*, Max Anders, Gen. Ed. Nashville, TN: Broadman & Holman Publishers. 2000.

Bruce, F.F. *Romans. Tyndale New Testament Commentaries* #6. Downers Grove, IL: InterVarsity Press. 1985.

Calvin, John. *Institutes of the Christian Religion*, Henry Beveridge, trans. Grand Rapids, MI: William B. Eerdmans Publishing Company. 1993.

The Christian History of the Constitution of the United States of America. Christian Self-Government. American Revolution Bicentennial Edition. Verna M. Hall, Compiler. San Francisco, CA: Foundation for American Christian Education. 1975.

The Christian History of the Constitution of the United States of America. Christian Self-Government With Union. American Revolution Bicentennial Edition. Verna M. Hall, Compiler. San Francisco, CA: Foundation for American Christian Education. 1987.

Eidsmoe, John. *Christianity and the Constitution. The Faith of Our Founding Fathers*. Grand Rapids, MI: Baker Book House. 1987.

Eidsmoe, John. *God and Caesar. Christian Faith & Political Action*. Westchester, IL: Crossway Books. 1984.

Federer, William J. *America's God and Country Encyclopedia of Quotations*. Coppel, TX: FAME Publishing, Inc. 1994.

Federer, William J. *Prayers and Presidents. Inspiring Faith From Leaders Of The Past*. St. Louis, MO: Amerisearch, Inc. 2010.

Foster, Marshall and Swanson, Mary-Elaine. *The American Covenant. The Untold Story*, Revised Ed. The Mayflower Institute. 1983.

God of Our Fathers. Advice and Prayers of Our Nation's Founders. Josiah Benjamin Richards, Editor. Reading, PA: Reading Books. 1994.

Gragg, Rod. *Forged in Faith. How Faith Shaped the Birth of the Nation 1607-1776*. New York: Howard Books. 2010.

James, Edgar C. *Romans, Amazing Grace!*, revised ed. Chicago: Moody Bible Institute. 1996.

Luther, Martin. *Commentary on Romans*, translated by J. Theodore Mueller. Grand Rapids, MI: Kregel Publications. 1992.

Marshall, Peter and Manuel, David. *From Sea to Shining Sea*. Tarrytown, NY: Fleming H. Revell Company. 1986.

Marshall, Peter and Manuel, David. *The Light and the Glory*. Grand Rapids, MI: Fleming H. Revell. 1977.

Marshall, Peter and Manuel, David. *Sounding Forth the Trumpet*. Grand Rapids, MI: Fleming H. Revell. 1997.

Millard, Catherine. *The Rewriting of America's History*. Camp Hill, PA: Horizon House Publishers. 1991.

Moo, Douglas J. *Romans. The NIV Application Commentary*. Grand Rapids, MI: Zondervan. 2000.

The New Encyclopedia of Christian Quotations. Mark Water – Compiler. Grand Rapids, MI: Baker Books. 2000.

One Nation Under God. A Celebration of America's Freedom. Darryl Shankle, Editor. Uhrichsville, OH: Barbour Publishing, Inc. 2003.

Robertson, Archibald Thomas. *Word Pictures in the New Testament, Volume IV, The Epistles of Paul.* Nashville, TN: Broadman Press. 1931.

Ryrie Study Bible, Expanded Edition. New American Standard Bible, 1995 Update. Chicago: Moody Press. 1995.

Schaeffer, Francis A. *A Christian Manifesto.* Grand Rapids, MI: Westchester, IL: Crossway Books. 1981.

Stott, John R.W. *The Message of Romans. God's Good News for the World. The Bible Speaks Today.* Downers Grove, IL: InterVarsity Press. 1994.

Vincent, Marvin R. *Word Studies in the New Testament, Volume III, the Epistles of Paul.* Peabody, MA: Hendrickson Publishers. n.d.

Zondervan NASB Study Bible. Kenneth Barker, General Editor. Grand Rapids MI: Zondervan Publishing House. 1999.

http://www.archives.gov/exhibits/charters/declaration_transcript.html

http://www.archives.gov/exhibits/charters/constitution_transcript.html

http://www.archives.gov/exhibits/charters/bill_of_rights_transcript.html

http://www.lonang.com/exlibris/rutherford/

http://www.wallbuilders.com/ - Wallbuilders

http://www.americanminute.com/ - William Federer

http://www.petermarshallministries.com/ - Peter Marshall Ministries

http://www.frc.org/ - Family Research Council

http://www.manhattandeclaration.org/home.aspx - The Manhattan
Declaration

http://www.principleapproach.org/ - The Foundation for American
Christian Education

http://www.afa.net/ - American Family Association

http://www.nrlc.org/ - National Right to Life Committee

http://onemillionmoms.com/ - One Million Moms

http://www.onemilliondads.com/ - One Million Dads

http://home.nra.org/ - National Rifle Association

http://www.hslda.org/ - Homeschool Legal Defense Association

http://www.eagleforum.org/ - Eagle Forum (Phyliss Schlafly)

http://aclj.org/ - American Center for law and Justice

http://www.answersingenesis.org/ - Answers in Genesis

http://www.freedomworks.org/ - Freedomworks

http://www.teapartypatriots.org/ - Tea Party Patriots

http://www.daveramsey.com/home/ - Dave Ramsey

http://narth.com/ - National Association for Research & Therapy of
Homosexuality

http://www.judicialwatch.org/ - Judicial Watch

For more information please contact:

Author's Email – turnthisnationaround@gmail.com

Author's FaceBook Page – Turn This Nation Around